KICKBOXING
SPARRING

KICKBOXING SPARRING

Justyn Billingham

THE CROWOOD PRESS

First published in 2009 by
The Crowood Press Ltd
Ramsbury, Marlborough
Wiltshire SN8 2HR

www.crowood.com

British Library Cataloguing-in-Publication Data
A catalogue record for this book is available from the British Library.

ISBN 978 1 84797 130 2

Disclaimer
Please note that the author and the publisher of this book are not responsible in any manner whatsoever for any damage or injury of any kind that may result from practising, or applying, the principles, ideas, techniques and/or following the instructions/information described in this publication. Since the physical activities in this book may be too strenuous in nature for some readers to engage in safely, it is essential that a doctor be consulted before undertaking training.

Throughout the text 'he', 'him' and 'his' are used as neutral pronouns and as such refer to both males and females.

Typeset and designed by D & N Publishing
Baydon, Wiltshire.

Printed and bound in Singapore by Craft Print International Ltd.

Contents

Dedication

I would like to dedicate this, my second book, to my wife, Sam,
an incredible person to whom I owe everything I have.

Acknowledgements

I would like to take this opportunity to thank a few people who have had a part to play in the development of my second book: David Mills from Cimac for supplying the uniforms and Adidas equipment featured in the book; my good friends and top instructors Nigel Sleath, Katie Pyle and Sarah Hunt, not only for their appearance in the book but also for all the help, support, dedication and commitment they have given me over the years; and finally my family for giving up yet another year of our lives so that I can make another dream a reality. I couldn't have done it without you.

Foreword

Just the other day I was in the mood for reminiscing and got out some old videos of my tournament career. As I flicked through one of them, a young Justyn Billingham popped up on it. Aged just 20, he was in with one of Britain's greatest ever fighters, the world welterweight champion Billy Bryce. I remember the fight well. Bryce was lightning quick and very clever, darting in and out, and even Billingham's renowned kicks were having trouble pinning him down. But, as you will no doubt gather from reading this book, a good fighter is a smart fighter. Billingham suddenly changed tack, switched tactics and 'Bam!', a single right hand stretched Bryce out on to his back.

Competitive combat, and sparring in preparation for it, go hand in hand with the practice of martial arts. After all, how else can you test out your techniques, your reflexes, your tactics and your timing without gloving up and throwing a bit of leather at a friend in class or at an opponent in the ring? Because of its importance, sparring has to be done just right. There is a fine, distinct art to it, and only a professional and experienced coach can give you the tools needed to spar, and fight, properly.

I was a two-time world champion in my early twenties for one good reason: I had good sparring. My coach, my own father, was an exceptional one.

And the guys at the gym with whom I was sparring, like Justyn Billingham, were all top-level fighters themselves. Justyn's incredible kicking ability was something I had to learn to deal with in every sparring session, and it stood me in good stead for when I later went out to the USA and had to confront some of the fantastic and powerful kickers they have over there.

If you have a good bunch of guys to practise your moves on, this book will act as your coach and help you to learn how to spar, and fight, properly!

Good luck!

Matt Winsper

Matthew Winsper
(NBL World Middleweight
Champion 1999; WPKA World
Light-Heavyweight Champion
2000; voted No.3 greatest
fighter of all time by
www.sportmartialarts.com)

1 Introduction

Sparring is the practice of controlled fighting using the techniques applicable to your chosen art form. Some arts refer to this stage of a student's training as 'playing', as that is precisely how you should approach a sparring session. Not to be confused with actual fighting, which is generally done when in competition (or of course in a self-defence situation), sparring involves the practice of attacking, defending and countering (the process of blocking and returning an attack) and brings into play all of the elements and principles of your martial arts training.

As such, sparring is the essence of the martial arts. It is the entity that brings together all the fundamentals of this once battlefield art and helps us to relive all the emotions, feelings and nuances that the warriors before us once experienced. To actually want to step into this world is, in itself, character building and it is often said that stepping onto the mats or into that cage or boxing ring is not dissimilar to stepping onto the battlefield or entering the gladiator's arena. Certainly, the risk factor is considerably reduced. There's a greater chance that we'll be walking back out again once the fight is over, but as we salute the mats before entering this environment we pay homage to all the warriors of the past and prove that their dedication to their cause, the intense training and honing of their skills and the development of some of the most incredible fighting arts we have in the world today, has lived on.

Too often I meet students who claim that they want to study a martial art, yet when it comes to sparring – the most important stage of their development – they 'bottle it', as the saying goes, and prefer not to enter this, the most exciting part of their training. It is a bit like learning to drive a car but being too nervous to take it out on the road; why bother learning to drive it at all? There are indeed a significant number of benefits that can be gained from studying kickboxing as a hobby, but those benefits may be gained from a number of other activities. The one thing that all the other sports, hobbies and pastimes cannot give you is the ability to learn how to defend yourself and possibly even one day save your life.

Punching pads, kicking shields and running around a dojo for hours on end will certainly help you lose weight, get fit and improve your flexibility, but this on its own is not enough to teach you how to fight. It is like training to be a footballer but never going out on to the field to play a match. The competitive situation is totally different from running around a training field all day, with so many other emotions and challenges to deal with and control. The pressure of competing at a higher intensity, where it suddenly matters if you are not concentrating one hundred per cent, changes everything and, although you will gain some health benefits from practising your punching and kicking whilst walking up and down the hall in lines all night, the only way you will ever actually learn how to fight is to *fight*.

It is often said that someone who is a black belt at punching pads becomes a white belt again once he puts on those boxing gloves and foot pads for the first time. Having the ability to stand almost toe to toe with someone, to hit them while they in turn try to hit you and you in turn try to avoid being hit, in any sporting way you can, takes immense dedication and skill. Developing this level of ability is not easy. It takes many years of training and dedication, and blood, sweat and tears to train your body up to the appropriate level. Even then, you may only just be touching the surface. To become good at it takes even longer and to become world class is only for the very special few.

Is it possible for absolutely anyone to become a world champion? I do not think so. We can all 'train like world champions' – and this is a phrase you will hear a lot over your years of training – but of course only a tiny minority will make it. In any case, for the majority, this is not what they really want, however, sparring and competitive fighting can still be a whole lot of fun. Not only that, but in my opinion nothing else comes remotely close to it for developing character. It can help to develop qualities in children that the media keeps reminding us are becoming rare in today's society. Strangely, learning to punch someone in the face in a controlled, sporting environment seems to prevent people from doing it for real out on the streets.

After writing a book on the technical aspect of kickboxing, my next logical step was to write one on sparring and competitive fighting. Most people who enter into the world of martial arts, particularly kickboxing (which is considered more of a sport than a martial art), will at some point try their hand at sparring. Some might simply test the water, realize it is a bit too cold, dry their feet and continue sunbathing. Some will wade in deeper and a few will dive straight in without any fear. It is definitely worth having a proper try and giving it your best shot.

For those who are just starting off on their adventure into the incredible world of kickboxing or martial arts and are curious about the secrets and mysteries of sparring – and maybe even, at some point, competitive fighting – this book is for them. Although the book is aimed predominately at the kickboxer, anyone who uses a kick or a punch as part of his fighting arsenal will be able to make use of the drills. In addition, as my background involves taekwon-do and karate as well as kickboxing and some reality-based arts, anyone studying these incredible sporting martial arts will gain some benefit from the following chapters.

The first time you take a punch and realize you are not made of glass; the first time your kick connects with someone and it does nothing to them; the first time you spar for just one minute and realize it is the most physically demanding thing you have ever done; these are all momentous occasions. If you have been there already you will know exactly what I mean. If not, then you are about to encounter one of the more rewarding activities in your personal development that you are ever likely to experience.

Now glove up and let's get started!

2 Solo Warm-Up Drills

Whatever your chosen sport, hobby, activity or pastime, if it involves some kind of physical exercise, you will hopefully understand how important the warm-up is. Without this stage of your training, however you choose to incorporate it, failing to warm your body up properly can have some serious consequences.

When I explain about warming up the body to my junior students, I use the analogy of an elastic band. If you take an elastic band and stretch it as far as you can there comes a point at which it will snap. If you warm up the elastic band a little first, though, the chances are that it will last longer before snapping. The analogy is even more convincing if you take the elastic band straight from the fridge and then stretch it. Because it is colder and therefore more brittle, it is likely to snap a lot sooner. Obviously, you do not warm up the body in order to take the muscles or tendons to a point at which they are likely to 'snap', but the elastic band example helps students understand how warming something up can help it to cope better when an increased force is applied to it.

The warm-up process needs to match the type of training you are about to do. In other words, there is not a great deal of point in warming up the body by focusing your attention on muscle groups and movements that you may not necessarily use in your chosen activity. Each sport will have its own preferred way of warming up the body to allow for the type of training its participants are about to undergo. For example a bodybuilder may not necessarily need to spend a great deal of time jogging around a running track prior to lifting heavy weights. A more experienced sports person will probably have their own warm-up routine, which they may have developed over the years,

having gained a good knowledge and experience of training in their field.

This is all covered by one simple phrase that I have adopted into my training vocabulary: 'Train for what you do.' So often people unnecessarily train in other sports or activities believing that doing this will complement their main sport or hobby. In fact, all they are doing is developing other skills that may not have any real influence over or enhance their main sport.

Incorporating weight-training into a non-weight-training-based activity is a good example. If done correctly, weights can be a great complement to an existing training programme and a huge number of athletes and sports people use weights in their training very successfully. However, weights can also be used incorrectly and, if you lack the real knowledge of how to lift weights properly in order to benefit your chosen sport, you may well find that, in the long run, you do yourself more harm than good. As with everything, a little knowledge can sometimes be quite dangerous, so make sure you know what you are doing from the start. If not, always seek the advice of an expert in that field.

The key thing to understand is that the warm-up is one of the most important parts of your training and that if you do not know how to warm up the body correctly, you may be increasing your risk of injury once you take your training to the next stage. Although you can never completely remove the risk of injury when working out, having a good in-depth knowledge of how to warm up and the various intensities involved will help to reduce this risk and ensure that you can look forward to a long and potentially injury-free training life.

There are a number of key benefits to warming up the body prior to exercise:

- release of adrenaline into the body, which helps to boost the supply of oxygen and glucose to the brain and muscles;
- increased heart rate, enabling oxygen in the blood to travel at a much faster speed to the muscles;
- increased production of synovial fluid located between the joints to reduce friction, which in turn allows the joints to move more efficiently;
- increase of temperature in the muscles, allowing for great elasticity of the muscle fibres and muscle contraction.

Warm-Up Drills

The following exercises are all good examples of how to warm up the body correctly for the type of kickboxing exercises that follow. They have been designed to start the process of warming up the body slowly and thoroughly, building up to full intensity over the correct amount of time and at the right pace and level. Once the warm-up is complete, conditioning exercises are incorporated to help strengthen the body as well as develop some of the core stabilizing muscles that the body uses to help with its movement and support.

Fig 1 (above left) Wrist rotation start position.

Fig 2 (above centre) Wrist rotation position 2.

Fig 3 (above right) Wrist rotation position 3.

Fig 4 (far left) Wrist rotation position 4.

Fig 5 (left) Wrist rotation finish position.

Fig 6 Open the hands, stretching out the fingers.

Fig 7 Clench the hands together tightly.

It will be worthwhile investing in a digital countdown timer (the type that can be found in most kitchen suppliers) or a large clock with a moving second hand. You will also find a digital countdown timer with audible beep useful later on in your training.

Solo Warm-Up Drills

Start with some simple warm-up drills that target specific areas of the body, can be done individually and require minimal space. These are ideal exercises if your training area is relatively small, for example, an occupied room in your house.

Warming up the Wrists

In a stationary position, feet shoulder-width apart, lightly clench your fists and start rolling both wrists in a circular motion from the inside out (in other words, right wrist in a clockwise motion and left wrist in an anti-clockwise motion). Do this ten times, rolling your wrists in a full circle each time, and then rotate them a further ten times in the other direction. Figs 1–5 show one complete revolution of the first wrist rotation drill.

Warming up the Hands

This time open up the hands as wide as possible, fully extending the fingers and holding for a second (Fig 6), before clenching the hands together into a fist as tightly as possible (Fig 7). Open and clench the hands ten times in total, working both hands at the same time.

Warming up the Arms and Shoulders

From the same position, stand with your hands down by your sides and start rotating both arms forwards in a circular motion, stretching as high as you can when your arms reach their highest point, and being certain to take them through the full range of motion. Do this twenty times in a forward direction and then twenty times in a backward direction.

If you are a more advanced student, try holding very light weights in the hands when you rotate the arms. This will add a little resistance to the exercise and result in a slightly more intense experience, which in turn will work the muscles a little harder. Be sure to rotate the arms very slowly when working with weights and use only very light weights for this stage of the warm-up. Figs 8 to 12

Fig 8 (above) Shoulder rotation start position.

Fig 9 (above centre) Shoulder rotation position 2.

Fig 10 (above right) Shoulder rotation position 3.

Fig 11 (right) Shoulder rotation position 4.

Fig 12 (far right) Shoulder rotation position 5.

show the full motion of the arms when rotated in this way.

Warming up the Shoulders and Chest
This time, to engage the chest into the routine a little, take your arms from the start position (Fig 13) across the body (Fig 14) and open once more (Fig 15). Repeat this exercise twenty times, taking the arms through the full movement of the exercise each time. This will ensure that the arms have

been moved in all directions and should remove any stiffness around the joints prior to the next stage of the training.

As before, the advanced student can use the same set of weights to take the intensity to a slightly higher level.

Warming up the Feet and Ankles
Finally, to complete the first stage of the warm-up and ensure that you are ready to start some

Fig 13 Chest and shoulder warm-up start position.

Fig 14 Chest and shoulder warm-up position 2.

Fig 15 Chest and shoulder warm-up finish position.

weight-bearing exercises, balance on one leg and raise your other foot off the ground slightly. Then, pointing your toes towards the floor, begin circling the foot in a clockwise direction for ten revolutions and then repeat the same exercise in an anti-clockwise direction for a further ten revolutions. Figs 16 to 19 show the full range of movement for this exercise.

Fig 16 Point the foot towards the floor.

Fig 17 Start rotating the foot to the ceiling.

Fig 18 Rotate the foot towards the side wall.

Fig 19 Rotate the foot back down towards the floor.

Fig 20 Start bouncing from your right foot.

Fig 21 To your left foot.

Increasing the Heartbeat

The body should now be better prepared for the next stage of the warm-up, where the aim is to get the heart pumping faster and increase the core temperature of the body, in preparation for the final stage of the warm-up. Again, start off slowly and introduce more intensity as you feel yourself getting warmer. Use your breathing to gauge the level of intensity that you should be applying at this stage. At no point should you be experiencing breathlessness. It is normal for your breathing and heart rate to increase slightly but you should still feel fairly comfortable at this stage in the warm-up.

Observing the breathing gives a good indication of a person's physical state during exercise, particularly when sparring. Someone who is breathing in through his nose will still have plenty of energy left in reserve. However, a person who is breathing in through his mouth during intense physical exercise is generally entering the final stages of his explosive aerobic ability before fatigue finally takes over and he has to either slow down or stop completely.

Warming up the Lower Body

Start off by raising yourself up on to the balls of your feet and gently bounce from one foot to the other (Figs 20 and 21). Although it is difficult to see this in the photographs, you ideally want to keep your heels off the floor at all times during this exercise and allow your arms to remain in a relaxed state down by your sides. Continue bouncing from foot to foot for around 30 seconds to 1 minute.

From here take the bounce up to a simple light jog, either on the spot or with movement. Unlike a traditional jog, however, with this variation your objective is to kick the legs up behind you, bringing the heel of each foot as high into the air as possible (Figs 22 and 23). As with a normal jog, keep the arms in close to the chest and try taking deep breaths in through your nose and out through your mouth, in order to control your breathing. Each time your left foot touches down, count one. When you reach twenty, change to the next exercise. Intermediate students can take this exercise up to fifty and advanced students can go up to seventy-five before changing to the following exercise.

Fig 22 Jogging on the spot, flicking your heels behind you.

Fig 23 Flicking the left heel behind you.

Fig 24 Place your hands out at waist level.

Continue jogging but now start bringing your knees up as high as you can, at least to waist height. Check that you are raising your knees high enough by placing your hands out in front of you (Fig 24) and ensuring that each time you bring your knee up it touches the appropriate hand (Fig 25). Again, aim for twenty per leg with an increase up to seventy-five for advanced students.

Finally, complete the lower-body warm-up by introducing the knee raise. This is a ballistic exercise that also serves a secondary purpose of stretching out the leg muscles slightly, which will in turn help to remove any stiffness of the legs and loosen off the joints in readiness for the stretching that will follow.

Start off by bouncing from foot to foot as you did for the first lower-body exercise. Once you have your rhythm, raise your left knee up as high as you can while continuing to bounce off the supporting leg. Each time the foot of the leg that you are raising touches down, use the floor as a springboard to bounce it back up again (Fig 26). Aim for ten repetitions with your left leg (fifteen for intermediate

Fig 25 Bring your knees up to your hands as you jog.

Fig 26 Bring your knee to your chest while hopping on the other foot.

Fig 27 Bring your knee to your shoulder while hopping on the other foot.

uninitiated may need a little time and persistence to develop it.

The key thing with skipping is to persevere with it regardless of how frustrating it might be when you first start. One piece of advice is to choose your rope wisely. The nylon-style ropes are generally affordable, long-lasting and able to cope with a multitude of speeds. It might also be worth considering a lightweight pair of training shoes (martial art shoes are ideal for this) to skip in if you have not skipped before, in case you catch your toes with the rope.

Those of you who can skip well, set your timer for 5 minutes and off you go. The rest of you, first make sure your rope is the right length. Stand on the middle of it and bring the handles up as high as they can go. If they reach your armpits then your rope is the correct size. If they fall short or are too high you will need a new rope.

Begin by simply hopping on one foot and then, rotating the rope using your wrists, attempt to pass it underneath the foot. Keep the hands and arms as

students and twenty for advanced) and then switch to your right leg.

Once you have completed the knee raises with each leg, change the exercise so you now bring the left knee up to the side of the body (Fig 27). Again, try bringing the leg up as high as you can, with an overall objective of touching the knee to the shoulder. As before, use the floor as a springboard to bring the knee straight back up again once it touches down and continue to bounce with a gentle rhythm using the supporting leg. Work ten repetitions on both sides, with an increase up to twenty for advanced students as before.

Warming up the Whole Body
By this stage of the warm-up you should be starting to feel slightly warmer, which is a good indication as to whether your core body temperature is increasing and, if so, at what pace. From here you can finish off the first stage of the warm-up with some skipping. Skipping is a great overall warm-up exercise, adopted by many of the fighting arts. However, skipping is a skill and the

Fig 28 Skipping.

Fig 29 Jump up just enough to pass the rope under your foot.

Fig 30 Bring your knee up high as you skip.

relaxed as possible in order to prevent lactic acid build-up in these areas and spin the rope using the wrists more so than the arms (Figs 28 and 29). Compare the position of the arms in Figs 28 and 29; you will see that they remain more or less static, despite the rope being in two different places.

You can also make this exercise more productive by hopping only high enough to allow the rope to pass under your foot. If you hop any higher you will use more energy and tire more quickly, increasing your chances of catching the rope and thus interrupting your rhythm. Once you feel the leg you are hopping on start to tire, switch legs without breaking your rhythm and repeat on the other side. Continue to switch between legs in this way, varying the time spent hopping on each leg as your skill in the art of skipping starts to improve.

More experienced skippers can try varying their footwork while they skip by incorporating movement – forwards and backwards, jogging on the spot, 5- to 10-second sprints, knee raises (Fig 30), heel and toe touches, and so on. This breaks up the rhythm and monotony of simply hopping from one foot to the other, which in turn will change your breathing pattern and help to make the exercise a bit more interesting.

3 Partner Warm-Up Drills

The following warm-up drills can be worked with a training partner and are ideally done after completing the basic solo warm-up (in other words, the initial part of the warm-up to the section on raising your heartbeat). The partner drills can then either be incorporated into your total warm-up routine so you complete all the drills contained in Chapter 2, or they can replace the second part of the solo warm-up routine (the section on raising your heartbeat), as they are also designed to raise your breathing and heartbeat and increase your overall core body temperature.

Alternatively, you may wish to mix up the drills so that you take a few from Chapter 2 and a few from Chapter 3, thereby varying your warm-ups to avoid the risk of boredom setting in through the monotony of training in exactly the same way at every session.

The truth is, there is no single perfect way to warm up. Everyone is different and an exercise that you enjoy or find easy to perform may be one at which your training partner is less skilled. As you become more experienced with the warm-up, you will no doubt be able to change or adapt certain drills to change and grow with you so you can ensure you are always pushing yourself to improve instead of remaining static.

Follow this simple guideline: when you can skip with ease for 2 minutes, increase it to 3 minutes.

Upright Rowing

Grip your partner's hands using your fingers to secure the hold. It does not really matter which way round your hands are but for the sake of understanding use an overhand grip with your left hand and an underhand grip with your right hand. Holding the arms at around chest height, slowly move the arms back and forth (*see* Figs 31 to 33). There are two possible options with this drill:

1. Start off slowly and increase the speed every 10 seconds for the duration of 1 minute ensuring that by the time you reach the final 10 seconds you are going as fast as you can.
2. Start off at a medium pace for 10 seconds and then increase the movement to full speed for between 5 and 10 seconds (depending on fitness and ability), reducing back to a medium pace for a further 10 seconds before repeating the drill once more. Alternate in this way for 1 minute, increasing the time in durations of 30 seconds as your fitness improves.

Fig 31 Working from an underhand overhand grip.

Fig 32 Move your arms back and forth.

Fig 33 To fully extended.

Jumps

There is a considerable amount of trust involved in the following sets of exercises so, if you are unsure about your jumping ability at this stage, it might be worth either missing the next few drills or using an inanimate object to jump over. A martial-art belt laid out on the floor would serve perfectly well, and you are unlikely to injure yourself on it should you miss your timing beat.

Leg Jumps

With your partner sitting down, position yourself to the side of their legs (Fig 34). Jump over their legs, bringing your knees up at the same time (as if doing a tuck jump) (Fig 35) and land on the other side (Fig 36). As soon as you land, jump straight back over to the other side and continue jumping from side to side in this way for either ten jumps, or for 1 minute (increasing the time or repetitions as you become more proficient at it).

Fig 34 Standing next to your partner.

Fig 35 Jump over their legs.

Twisting Leg Jumps

With your partner adopting the same position as the last drill, this time working from a left lead fighting stance, face the side wall as shown (Fig 37). Now as you jump, twist your body in midair (Fig 38), so that you end up facing the opposite side when you land but retain your left lead position (Fig 39). From here you can either jump back and reverse the motion or, from your landing position, you can jump once more, switching your legs in midair (Fig 40), and land back down facing the same direction but having just switched your lead (from left to right) (Fig 41).

If you opt to add in this extra jump, then repeat the twisting jump landing with your right leg in front this time and once again static jump to switch lead before reversing the drill. This drill might take a little time and practice to get right but it is worth persevering, as it will help to develop your ability to stay light on your feet as well as developing explosive power in the legs – two key things required for sparring and competitive fighting.

Fig 36 Landing on the opposite side.

Fig 37 In a staggered stance.

Fig 38 Jump into the air, turning the body.

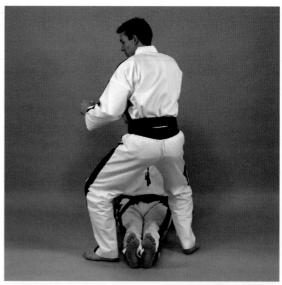

Fig 39 And landing on the opposite side.

Fig 40 Jump into the air.

Fig 41 Changing legs as you land.

Timing Jumps

This drill may well be the trickiest of the three and you will need to work in total harmony with your training partner in order to get it right. With your partner in the same position as before, start off with your legs straddling your partner's (Fig 42).

From a stationary position, jump into the air as high as you can, bringing your knees up to your body as if performing a tuck jump. At the same time, your partner opens his legs (this is where the timing element comes in to play) (Fig 43). As you land, be sure to land with your legs together, into the gap created by your partner (Fig 44).

As soon as you touch down, use the floor as a springboard and jump up as before with little to no pause, ensuring your partner closes his legs as you jump (Fig 45). Land back down again with your legs on either side of your partner's (Fig 46) and continue jumping in this way for either ten jumps or for 1 minute, increasing the time and

Fig 42 (above) Standing over your partner's legs.

Fig 43 (above centre) Jump into the air as your partner opens their legs.

Fig 44 (above right) Land in the centre.

Fig 45 (right) Jump into the air again.

Fig 46 (far right) Land straddling their legs.

repetitions as you become more proficient with the drill.

These drills are not only great for helping to warm up the body but also help to develop other skills essential for sparring and competitive fighting, such as agility, balance, explosive speed, leg strength, timing and movement. On top of this they are quite good fun to perform with a (competent) training partner.

Sparring Drills

The next set of partner warm-up drills will require you to put your sparring equipment on. We'll take a look at what you will require to reduce the risk of injury when entering this stage of your training in the box at the end of this chapter. A good piece of advice here is to put on the bare minimum prior to starting your warm-up, as this will reduce both the time you take to 'kit up' and the time you spend cooling down.

For the less experienced sparring student, getting your sparring kit on can take some considerable time as you work out what needs to go where and how it all does up, so by starting off

with footpads, shin pads and, if possible, even groin guards on ensures you are halfway there and cuts the cooling down time in half, if not more.

It is important to remember that you are still warming up the body so it is advisable to reduce the speed, energy, power and intensity of the following drills until after completion of this stage. Remember to work with your partner and not against them; your job here is to ensure that your partner gets as much out of the drills as you do.

One-for-One Punching

Face one another in a fighting stance (Fig 47) and, working slowly and carefully, attempt to tag your partner using all the basic punches that you know (jab, cross, hooks, uppercuts, backfists, and so on). Work the drill in turn using just one punch at a time – you punch, then your partner punches, then you punch again, and so on. Start off working for 1 minute and increase the drill to a maximum of 2 minutes as you become more proficient at it. Figs 48 to 51 demonstrate this drill.

There are a number of alternative options with this drill:

• using one-for-one punches, target the body only;

Fig 47 Facing your partner in the same lead.

Fig 48 Punch to the body.

Fig 49 Your partner returns the attack.

Fig 50 You attack again.

Fig 51 Your partner attacks again.

- using one-for-one punches, target the head only;
- using one-for-one punches, target the head and the body randomly;
- isolate specific punches and use only this punch to attack with;

- attempt to block the attack from your partner;
- allow the punches to land;
- remain stationary throughout;
- add in movement thus incorporating footwork into the drill.

One-for-One Kicking

Continue the same drill as before but using just the round kick and aiming for your partner's thigh this time. As you have not stretched the leg muscles up to this point it is important to keep the kicks quite low, to reduce the risk of injury from over-extending the joint or exceeding the kicking range at this early stage in the warm-up. As before, work this drill for 1 minute, increasing to 2 minutes once you get more comfortable with the exercise. To start with, work in the same lead as your partner and just isolate the lead round kick, attacking your partner's inner thigh area (Figs 52 and 53).

For the next round, isolate your rear leg attacking to the outer area of your partner's thigh only (Figs 54 and 55). Then, if you feel up to it, add in a minute of attacking either the inner or outer thigh using your lead and rear leg accordingly. As you feel your legs start to warm up with the kicking movement, and the tendons begin to stretch out a little, take the kicks up to the mid level for

Fig 52 You kick to the legs.

Fig 53 Your partner kicks to the legs.

Fig 54 Kick off your rear leg to the legs.

Fig 55 Your partner kicks off his rear leg, targeting your legs.

Fig 56 Kick off your lead leg to the body.

Fig 57 Receive a kick to the body.

Fig 58 Rear-leg kick to the body.

Fig 59 Receive a rear-leg kick to the body.

Fig 60 Lead-leg kick to the head.

Fig 61 Rear-leg kick to the head.

an additional round, kicking with either the instep (Figs 56 and 57) or the shin (Figs 58 and 59).

Finally, and only if you feel you are warmed up enough at this stage, and your natural flexibility allows the movement, take the kicks up to the head. Use the lead leg (Fig 60) and the rear leg (Fig 61). Complete the drill by randomly kicking to the leg, body or head using the round kick one for one.

Equipment

Men – From Top to Bottom

Head Guard
A good-quality head guard, with padding on the top as well as the sides and rear, is of the utmost importance. Many head guards, such as some used in boxing, are not padded on the top, because, as a rule, boxers do not punch to the top of the head. However, in kickboxing (and other kicking arts), participants are susceptible to downward attacks such as those delivered by an axe kick, and it is essential to have a head guard that protects this delicate area.

Make sure that the head guard does not move when it gets hit. Equipment made of dipped foam has a tendency to slip once the wearer starts to sweat, as the material becomes frictionless. It also has a tendency to rip or tear over time and use, which can be quite dangerous given the nature of what it is designed to do. Many schools no longer allow dipped-foam equipment because of this risk. The head guard also needs to protect the head if it hits the floor, should the wearer slip or fall over, so it is worth investing in a good-quality one.

Fig 62 Equipment required for sparring – men.

Gum Shield

The gum shield's job is to protect the teeth and sparring should not be done without one. The price varies considerably, from a few pounds for an over-the-counter one to much more for a professionally fitted dental version. It must be moulded correctly, following the instructions that will come with it. In most cases a single gum shield (covering the top set of teeth) will suffice; for additional protection, a double gum shield will protect both the upper and lower teeth.

Boxing Gloves

Hand protection is important, and training partners owe it to each other to wear the correct glove for the type of sparring they are about to undergo. As a basic rule, continuous sparring generally involves the use of boxing gloves and these range from 8oz up to 16oz, with gloves used in competitive sparring generally being around 10–12oz.

As with everything, there are many different makes and styles of boxing glove, and a wide range of prices. For quick fitting and removal, consider a glove with a velcro fastener as the tie-up ones require a little more time and patience (and help) to get on and off.

Groin Guard

Groin guards are generally worn underneath the clothing (the one in the photograph is worn over the trousers just so that it can be seen). A deluxe style (oversized) groin guard will offer a greater level of protection than a cricket-box-style groin guard. Obviously, serious injury could result from a strike or connection in this area of the body, so it is certainly worth considering a guard that offers the highest level of protection.

Shin Guard

Shin guards are designed to eliminate the bone-on-bone contact experienced when kicks clash as well as offering protection to your partner should you connect with your shin (either intentionally or accidentally). There are many different styles of shin pad available; look for one that protects the whole of the shin, both length and width, as well as gripping well (*see* page 30 for information on dipped-foam material). Velcro straps allow for quick fitting and removal, while the elasticated, sock-style guards do tend to lose their elasticity over time.

Foot Pads

Foot pads are the final essential requirement and are predominately designed to protect your partner, with a secondary benefit of protecting your own foot against accidental kicks to the elbow and the like. There are many different foot pads available and the styles ideal for kickboxing training offer complete protection of the top, sides and rear of the foot.

Foot pads are designed to be worn with bare feet. The boot-style ones (*see* the photograph) slide on like a shoe and generally have toe straps to ensure that the toes are not exposed, as well as an additional fixing strap that wraps around the boot in a figure of eight, securing the pad tightly to the foot. Just be aware that foot pads generally leave the underside of the foot exposed, for improved grip, so, in the case of strikes with the ball of the foot or the underside of the heel, they offer no protection to your partner.

Women

The equipment requirements for women (Fig 63) mirror those for men, with the alternative option of a female groin protector, which will give added protection and peace of mind.

Body Protection

Body armour is a further optional extra that might be worth considering, to give added protection to the body (male or female), regardless of how well conditioned the abdominal muscles may be. It is always a good idea to keep yourself as fully protected as possible and this item will give added protection to the chest area, which is particularly important for the female fighter.

Additional Items

Additional items of protection worth considering include elbow protectors and knee pads. The elbows and knees are not generally used in kickboxing so the benefit will be felt only when you fall over or when your partner accidentally kicks or punches this area. Landing on an elbow can be extremely painful as well as damaging to the joint, and a good-quality pad that protects this area will reduce the risk of injury. The same applies to the knees.

Fig 63 Equipment required for sparring – women.

4 Conditioning Drills

The conditioning drills are to be done only after fully completing the warm-up stage (either solo or partner). They are designed to condition the body, in order to strengthen it, and in turn to improve your ability to receive an attack should you fail to block it. They will also help to develop the core muscles within the body and this in turn will help you to improve your ability to deliver faster and more powerful attacks in return. They will also help you improve your stamina and fitness, which is essential if you are to last any length of time in sparring or a competitive fight.

Vary the number of exercises you begin with, based on your current levels of fitness and stamina. As a rough guide, if you are new to this, attempt between five and ten of each exercise. Intermediate-level students can attempt between ten and twenty and advanced students may wish to attempt between twenty and thirty to begin with. As your fitness and stamina increase, so you can increase the number of repetitions. Do not attempt to increase by too many reps. If you are just managing to perform ten repetitions of any exercise, for example, it is going to be nearly impossible for you to add an extra five. Just step it up one rep at a time and make sure that you keep good technique and form throughout each exercise, rather than 'cheating' and sacrificing form and quality for speed and reps.

The Star Jump

The star jump is a general conditioning exercise used to develop the whole body at a lower intensity.

Stamina or Fitness?

People often confuse the terms 'stamina' and 'fitness' and therefore fail to develop these key attributes properly or even understand what they mean. The general rule is that 'fitness' refers to the body's ability to recover after a burst of exercise, whereas 'stamina' refers to the length of time for which the person can sustain that exercise, at a certain level of intensity.

The term 'stamina' is often used in relation to running, suggesting that the more stamina a runner has, the faster, harder and further they can run. The same is true with the fighter – the better his stamina, the further he can push himself and the longer he can last.

The term 'fitness' is used to describe a person's ability to recover or, in simpler terms, to catch their breath. The fitter you are, the quicker you can recover and the harder you can work when you begin your next set of exercises. For example, after 3 minutes of sparring, a boxer generally gets a minute to rest and recover before starting again. The fitter that boxer is, the less time he needs to catch his breath before starting the next round.

Fig 64 Start position for the star jump.

Fig 65 Mid-air position for the star jump.

It is an excellent conditioning exercise, particularly for the beginner, and in some cases can be used as part of a warm-up. The general rule with a star jump is to go from a stationary position (Fig 64), jump into the air (Fig 65) and bring your hands above your head, landing with your feet apart (Fig 66) before jumping back to your start position.

The Push-Up

The push-up is a great exercise for developing upper-body strength. From the starting position

Fig 67 Start position for the push-up.

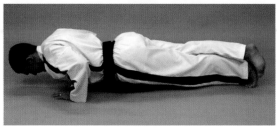

Fig 68 Midway position for the push-up.

Fig 66 Finish position for the star jump.

Fig 69 Finish position for the push-up.

(Fig 67), lower the body down so that the chest just touches the floor without collapsing (Fig 68) and push back up, locking out the arms (Fig 69). A slight variation on the standard push-up is done by crossing the feet as shown.

There are a number of other variations on the push-up:

- arms shoulder width apart – ensure the hands are in line with the chest (Figs 70 and 71);
- elbows close – ensure the elbows are kept in close to the body throughout the whole of the push-up (Figs 72 and 73);
- close grip – bring the hands together so that the thumbs and fingers touch directly underneath the chest. Bring the chest down on to the hands

Fig 70 Variation on the push-up with arms at shoulder width.

Fig 71 The midway point.

Fig 72 Push-up with elbows close in to the body.

Fig 73 The midway point.

Fig 74 Close-grip push-up.

Fig 75 The halfway point.

and push back up again without collapsing (Figs 74 and 75);

- clapping push-ups – perform a standard push-up as normal then, on returning to the upright position, push your body off the floor using an explosive movement and clap the hands together before landing (Fig 76);
- jumping push-ups – as above but, as you push back up, jump off the floor, bringing your whole body (hands and feet) off the ground at the same time (Fig 77);
- chest touch – push up as normal and, as you come back up to the start position, bring your right arm up to the body followed by your left arm on your next push-up (Figs 78 to 82);
- one-arm push-ups – form a triangle using your

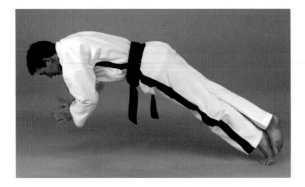

Fig 76 Clapping push-up.

Fig 77 Jumping push-up.

Fig 78 Chest-touch push-up start position.

Fig 79 Lower the body to the floor.

Fig 80 Come back up to the start position.

Fig 81 Pull the right arm back in to the body.

legs and one arm for balance and lower your chest to the floor pushing back up again using just one arm (Figs 83 and 84);

- ladies' push-ups – from a standard push-up position, lower your knees to the floor. Bring your body down as normal and push back up again in the usual way (Figs 85 to 86). Alternatively cross your feet (Fig 87).

The Sit-Up

As with the push-up, there are many ways to perform a sit-up, and several variations of the exercise. All are designed to develop the abdominal region, strengthening the core and creating that much-coveted 'six pack', where the main rectus abdominus muscles are well defined. (This look will not

Fig 82 Pull the left arm up into the body.

Fig 83 One-arm push-up start position.

Fig 84 Bring the chest down to the floor.

Fig 85 Ladies' push-up start position.

Fig 86 Bring your chest down to the floor.

Fig 87 Feet crossed over.

be achieved, however, by hundreds of repetitions alone if there is a layer of fat, however small, covering those muscles; a good understanding of diet is important too.) In fact, everyone has their own 'six pack' – otherwise we would be unable to hold ourselves up – and it is vital for the kickboxer to learn how to develop the upper, lower and side (oblique) muscles, as this will greatly assist in protecting the inner organs from injury and go a long way towards developing stability of the core.

Standard Sit-Up

Lie on your back with your knees bent, shoulders off the floor and fingers touching your temples. Raise the body up towards the knees using the abdominal muscles alone (Figs 88 and 89). Be sure not to take your fingers off your temples or use your arms in any way to assist and make the movement easier and, as you lower your body back down, be sure to keep the shoulders off the floor.

Fig 88 Standard sit-up start position.

Fig 89 Raise your body up to your knees.

Butterfly Sit-Up

This version is aptly named due to the position of the legs throughout the exercise. Keep your legs open, chin on your chest and arms by your sides and raise the body up as high as you can. Hold for a count of 3 seconds and then lower back down (Figs 90 and 91).

Fig 90 Butterfly sit-up start position.

Fig 91 Raise your body up as high as you can.

Crunches

Position yourself as for a standard sit-up but this time bring your feet off the floor. You will need to find your balance point before you start the movement. Bring the knees and elbows together in the middle and return to the start position. Keep the shoulders and legs off the floor at all times (Figs 92 and 93).

'V' Sit-Ups

Lie flat on the floor with your arms outstretched behind your head. Bring your arms and feet together in the middle and lower back down (Fig 94 and 95).

Fig 92 Start position for the crunch sit-up.

Fig 93 Bring your knees and elbows together.

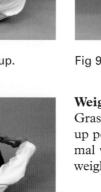

Fig 94 Start position for the 'V' sit-up.

Weighted Sit-Ups

Grasp a weight plate as shown in the standard sit-up position and perform standard sit-ups as normal with the extra resistance. You can also use a weighted jacket if you have one (Figs 96 and 97).

Burpees

The burpee is an incredibly effective all-over body-conditioning exercise but it is not for the faint-hearted. It is a very tough exercise and because of this there are a couple of versions to try.

For a half burpee, start in an upright position, bend over and touch your toes and then spring up

Fig 95 Bring your hands and feet together.

Fig 96 Weighted sit-up.

Fig 97 Sit back, keeping the shoulders off the floor.

Fig 98 (top left) Bend forwards from the waist.

Fig 99 (top centre) Jump up into the air, forming a star shape.

Fig 100 (top right) Start position for the full burpee.

Fig 101 (centre left) Place the hands on the floor.

Fig 102 (centre) Kick back with the legs.

Fig 103 (left) Bring the legs back to a squat position.

Fig 104 (right) Spring up into the air.

into the air, performing a mid-air star jump. As you land, immediately return to the bent over position and repeat the exercise (Figs 98 and 99).

For a full burpee, from the upright position, bend over and drop your hands to the floor, kicking the legs back as if performing a squat thrust. Keep low to the ground and bring the legs back in towards your elbows. From this squat position, drive yourself up and off the floor performing the mid-air star jump as before (Figs 100 to 104).

Lunges

Lunges are used for developing strength in the legs and as with the burpee there is an easy way and a hard way to do them.

For a simple lunge, start in an upright position, and keep your hands on your hips to prevent the temptation of pushing yourself back up to your stationary position by placing your hands on your legs. Step forward, alternating between

Fig 105 (top left) Simple lunge start position.

Fig 106 (top right) Step forwards with the left leg.

Fig 107 (bottom left) Jumping lunge.

Fig 108 (bottom right) Land with the other leg forward.

legs and push back to your start position (Figs 105 and 106).

The slightly more advanced version involves a jump taking you from your forward lunge position with your left leg forward to your forward lunge position with your right leg forward. There is no need to return to the start position in between (Figs 107 to 108).

Tuck Jumps

Tuck jumps are another good exercise for developing lower-body strength. Flexibility can be a issue with this one. Ideally you need to get your knees up to your body and this is something that many people struggle with. Focus on jumping as high as you can and bringing your knees to at least

Fig 109 (top left) Tuck jump start position.

Fig 110 (top centre) Jump into the air, bringing your knees to the chest.

Fig 111 (top right) Place the fingers on the temples.

Fig 112 (bottom left) Bend down so the elbows touch the knees.

Fig 113 (bottom right) Jump up into the air.

Fig 114 Lie on your front with your fingers on your temples.

Fig 115 Raise your body up as high as you can.

Fig 116 Bring your feet and body off the floor together.

waist height in order to benefit from this exercise.

For a simple tuck jump, from a standing position, jump into the air as high as you can and bring your knees up to your chest at your highest point (Figs 109 to 110).

For a more advanced version, start with your fingers on your temples. Bend your legs, bringing your elbows down to your knees, and from this squat position jump up into the air, keeping your fingers on your temples and trying to touch your knees to your elbows in mid-air (Figs 111 to 113).

Hyperextension

This is a great conditioning exercise for the lower back, an area of the body that can be easily neglected.

For a simple hyperextension, lie on your front with your fingers on your temples and lift your upper body off the floor, attempting to look up at the ceiling (Figs 114 to 115).

A more advanced variation involves bringing your feet off the floor at the same time as bringing your body off the floor. The best way to explain the movement required for this version is to imagine trying to touch the feet to the back of the head (Fig 116).

5 Partner Conditioning Drills

If you have a training partner to work with, partner conditioning drills can either complement or replace solo drills. Working in this way is great for developing your training further as a training partner can offer encouragement, support and assistance throughout the exercises. If you add an element of competition to this stage of your training, you may also find that you are able to push yourself further than you might otherwise have pushed yourself had you been training alone.

This is also true for anyone training in a class environment. Often, the martial art student, keen to make an impression or not wanting to be seen to finish an exercise last, will sacrifice good technique or even choose not to complete the required number of repetitions of a certain exercise or training drill. A good training partner can help to prevent this kind of bad habit from forming and ensure that all the exercises are completed correctly.

Push-Up Drills

The following drills are great examples of how a training partner can assist with key conditioning exercises such as the push-up. Try working the following drills using the fitness guide mentioned in

---

Good Foundations

Remember: good foundations are the key to martial arts. Cutting corners at the early stages will lead to bad habits. The stronger your foundations, the stronger your martial arts. It is just like building a house. The stronger the foundations, the more chance the house has of weathering a storm. Weak foundations will eventually result in the house collapsing and it will probably happen when you need it the most.

Chapter 4 to give you a realistic target, based on your current level of fitness.

Partner Assisted Push-Up
From your standard push-up position, instruct your training partner to place their fist underneath your chest (Fig 117). From here, lower the

Fig 117 Place your fist under the chest.

Fig 118 Bring the chest down to touch the fist.

body down until you feel your chest touch your partner's fist (Fig 118). Be sure not to collapse at this point and, using your chest and arms, push your body back up again to its start position. Repeat straight away with no pause, but be careful not to perform the repetitions too fast as this tends to mean that momentum rather than strength is being used to effect each movement, making the exercise easier to do.

To add an element of competition to this drill, have your partner count each time your chest touches their fist. If the chest fails to touch the fist, that rep is not counted. Continue until you are no longer able to complete a full rep and then switch places with your partner. Your partner then has to try to beat your score. Alternate between being the

pacemaker and the second person and, as you get better and stronger at performing this drill, add a time limit in (as many push-ups as you can do in 60 seconds, for example).

Incline Push-Up
For this drill your partner kneels down and you place your feet on their back, supporting yourself with your arms (*see* Fig 119). From here, drop your chest down, making sure you touch the chest to the floor (Fig 120), then push straight back up to your start position.

Advanced Incline Push-Up
This exercise is similar to the incline push-up, but your partner raises himself slightly, thereby

Fig 119 Place your feet on your partner's back.

Fig 121 Increase the height.

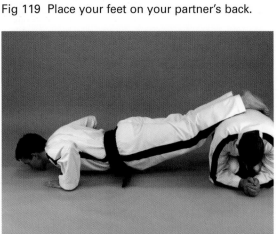

Fig 120 Bring your chest down to the floor.

Fig 122 Bring your chest down to the floor.

increasing the distance between your chest and the floor. Figs 121 and 122 show how to perform this exercise correctly. Be sure to bring the chest to the floor as before, otherwise you run the risk of performing only half of the exercise.

Inverted Push-Up

This one is probably the most advanced type of push-up and will require some considerable upper-body strength. You also need to make sure you have a training partner whom you trust and one who can fully support you throughout the whole movement of this exercise. The easiest way to set up the position is for you to start off in a standard push-up position and have your partner lift your legs off the floor. To ensure that they have a good grip, they wrap their arms around your ankles as shown and check that they have their balance set correctly (Fig 123). As before, drop your chest down to the ground (Fig 124) and, using your upper-body strength, push back up to your start position.

Sit-Up Drills

These are performed in the same way as the push-up drills, by working to your fitness level and ensuring you use good form throughout.

Standard Sit-Up

With your partner in a sit-up position, place your body so that you are sitting on their feet locking their legs in place, and hold your hands out in front of you (Fig 125). From this start position, your partner now needs to raise themselves up using their abdominal muscles only and touch your hands as shown (Fig 126). From here they lower themselves back down, ensuring they keep their shoulders off the floor, in order to keep the tension on the abdominal muscles and develop this area.

Putting your shoulders on the floor each time releases the tension on the abdominal muscles and therefore fails to develop these muscles correctly. As soon as they feel their lower back touch the floor, they need to repeat the exercise until they reach their set number. Swap and repeat the drill.

Fig 123 Hold your partner's legs.

Fig 124 Bring your chest down to the floor.

Fig 125 Sit on the feet and hold your hands out.

Fig 126 Sit up and touch hands.

Advanced Sit-Up

Lie on your back and bend your knees. Have your partner sit on your knees (they will need to find their balance point) and tuck their feet under your shoulders. Wrap your arms around their legs for additional support (Fig 127). From here they lower their upper body down to about a 45-degree angle (Fig 128) and, using their abdominal muscles, raise back up to approximately 90 degrees (just short of their start position). Be careful not to come too far forward with this exercise as this will release the tension on the stomach. A common cheat with this is to bend too far forward, so each participant should ensure that their partner uses correct form throughout. As your strength with this one improves you can try lowering down even further. Just be careful not to overdo it at the start.

Fig 127 Sit on your partner's knees as they support your legs.

Fig 128 Lean back to start the sit-up.

Standing Sit-Ups

The key with this exercise is your ability to support your partner and this in itself is quite a skill involving considerable teamwork. With your partner in an upright position, wrap your legs around theirs and support the backs of their legs as shown (Fig 129). Ensure you are holding on to them tightly so they cannot fall.

From here your partner bends their legs and lowers their body to the floor (Fig 130), then lies back (Fig 131) and performs one full sit-up using their abdominal muscles (Fig 132). As soon as they have performed the sit-up, they use the strength in their legs and abdominal muscles to lift their whole body back off the floor again (Fig 133) and stand up (Fig 134). They repeat the whole movement for a second time and continue

Fig 129 Stand up as your partner secures your legs.

Fig 130 Bend your legs.

Fig 131 Sit down.

Fig 132 Perform a sit-up.

Fig 133 Start to stand.

Fig 134 Complete the exercise.

until they have reached their target number (or until muscular failure, depending on how you are choosing to perform your conditioning drills at this stage).

Other Partner-Assisted Conditioning Drills

Try incorporating the following drills into your training routine to further develop your core strength as well as your overall body conditioning. Either work these drills alongside the previous ones or as an alternative to them, based on your time constraints and/or your fitness levels.

Partner-Assisted Burpees

Stand facing your partner, holding your hands out in front of you (Fig 135). Your partner performs a full burpee in the normal way (Figs 136 to 139) but, as they jump into the air, they need to ensure that they touch your hands to complete the exercise properly. The greater the fitness level of your partner, the higher you hold your hands, encouraging your partner to jump as high as they can every time.

Fig 135 Face your partner with your hands held high.

Fig 136 Start the burpee.

Fig 137 Kick your legs back.

Fig 138 Return to a squat position.

Fig 139 Jump and touch hands.

Fig 140 Stand with your hands out in front.

Fig 141 Jump and touch your knees to your partner's hands.

Partner-Assisted Tuck Jumps

Stand facing each other and instruct your partner to hold their hands out at a level you are comfortable with (Fig 140). Using the traditional tuck jump method, spring as high into the air as you can, touching your knees to your partner's hands (Fig 141). Try to ensure you jump straight back up after landing, avoiding the common cheat of double-jumping in between each rep.

Partner-Assisted Hyperextensions

The final conditioning exercise uses the hyperextension, which is a core exercise for developing the lower back. It is common to neglect this area of the body and instead focus solely on developing areas such as the chest and abdominal muscles. However, the back is an incredibly important area to develop, as a weak back can potentially lead to problems in later life, particularly if it undergoes the stresses of a training programme with no real focus on its own development.

Lie on your front and instruct your partner to sit on the lower part of your legs. Place your fingertips on your temples (Fig 142) and at the same time raise the body up as high as you can off the floor (Fig 143). Once you have reached your

Fig 142 With your partner on their front, sit at the base of their legs.

Fig 143 Raise up as high as you can.

highest point, bring the chest back down again and immediately raise the body up once more. Continue until you reach your target or until muscular failure.

Weighted Hyperextension

You should perform this final conditioning exercise only if you are able to hit your target with ease on the last exercise and your lower back is strong enough to withstand the additional resistance you

Adding Resistance

Extra weight can be incorporated into almost all of the conditioning exercises that do not involve explosive movement of any kind. As demonstrated in some of the previous drills (such as the weighted sit-up, *see* page 38, and the weighted hyperextension), the addition of weight helps to develop and condition the body even further.

A weighted jacket makes the addition of external weight easier than trying to hold a free weight in the hands or balance one on the body (for example, on the back when performing a push-up). If you do decide to invest in a weighted jacket, buy a good-quality one. There are some poor versions on the market that will not last long, and expensive does not necessarily mean good. Check that the stitching is firm and make sure that the jacket can be adjusted to fit the body tightly, as this will prevent it from dragging on the floor when used for exercises such as push-ups and sit-ups, or bouncing around if used for running.

will be using. Supporting a light weight with your hands behind the back of your head (Fig 144), and once again raise your body off the floor as far as you can before gently lowering down and repeating (Fig 145).

With the external weight being employed, great care must be taken to make your movement slow and deliberate and avoid any jerky or sudden movements. You should also start off with a very light weight and build up the resistance gradually over time. A good guide is to work this one until muscular failure, note the number and, when you can exceed this number with ease, slightly increase the weight.

Fig 144 For an advanced version, place a weight behind your head.

Fig 145 Raise up as high as you can.

6 Stretching and Flexibility Training

There is much scientific theory related to stretching and many books have been written on the subject. The key exercises described here will help develop your flexibility and ensure that you complete the warm-up stage of your training correctly. Often, students neglect flexibility training due to its intensity and a lack of knowledge and understanding in the area. However, without an adequate level of leg flexibility, kicking can be very difficult to perform and, human nature being what it is, students can become easily demoralized and miss out, or perhaps not work quite as hard as they should in this specific area.

Stretching should be a relatively pleasant experience. You should stretch to the point at which you can feel it but it should in no way be causing any pain. If you do experience pain of any kind while you perform the following stretching drills, you are probably doing too much. Simply ease off slightly to reduce the sensation and continue at a level with which you are comfortable.

The human body is quite resilient and you can be reassured that you would need to push it quite considerably (if training incorrectly) before doing any serious damage. Therefore, as long as you are careful with your stretching, you listen to your body (pain is the body's way of telling you to stop doing something) and you do not do any sudden or explosive movements, you should reduce the risk of any injury occurring and ensure that you have a long and healthy journey in the world of stretching and flexibility training.

Upper-Body Stretching

Begin by stretching out the upper body, to ensure that the neck, shoulders, arms and waist are sufficiently loosened. This is an area that can often be overlooked when stretching, as emphasis is nearly always placed predominately on the lower body. For all the stretching drills contained within this section, hold for approximately 10 seconds before changing.

Loosening the Neck
In a standing position, with your legs approximately shoulder-width apart, cup the left side of your head using your right hand. From here gently pull the head across to the right until you feel the stretch on the left side of the neck (Fig 146). Repeat on the other side.

Using both hands, cup the back of the head and gently pull the head down towards the chest (Fig 147).

Place the fingertips lightly on the forehead. Keep the mouth open and gently push the head back to look up at the ceiling (Fig 148).

Finally, cup the chin in the left hand and place the right hand on the back of the head. Very gently twist the head to the left side until you feel the stretch, then repeat on the other side (Fig 149).

Loosening the Shoulders
Standing with your feet approximately shoulder width apart, take your right arm across your body and, using the left arm to support, cup the arm just above the elbow using the bicep and the forearm. Pull back with the left arm until you feel the stretch on your right shoulder. Repeat on the other side (Fig 150).

Point to the ceiling with your right arm and bend from the elbow, keeping the lower part of your arm straight. Grab your right elbow using your left hand and gently push your arm as far down your back as you can get it (Fig 151). Repeat on the other side.

Fig 146 (top left) Gently pull the head across to the right.

Fig 147 (top centre) Gently pull the head forwards.

Fig 148 (top right) Gently pull the head backwards.

Fig 149 (bottom left) Gently twist the head to the left.

Fig 150 (bottom centre) Stretch your right arm across your body.

Fig 151 (bottom left) Stretch your right arm down your back.

Fig 152 Bend over to the left.

Fig 153 Drop your body down towards the floor.

Fig 154 Lean back and push your hips forwards.

Loosening off the Waist

In a shoulder-width stance, point to the ceiling with your right hand. Bend over to the left side taking your right hand over your head until you can feel the stretch on the right side of your body (Fig 152). Repeat on the other side.

Return to your start position and now lean forwards keeping your hips where they are and attempt to relax and hang into the centre (Fig 153).

Finally, come back up to your start position and place your hands on your hips, with your thumbs into the lower back. Push your hips forwards with your hands, leaning back as you do so. Keep your mouth open and your legs straight and attempt to look at the back wall (Fig 154). Be careful not to over-balance.

Lower-Body Stretching

The following stretching drills will help to develop flexibility in the legs, which in turn should greatly improve kicking ability. The key thing to understand with stretching for this purpose is to do it often. Just once or twice a week is probably not enough for the average person to notice much

of an improvement; failing to see instant results is one of the reasons why people can get disheartened and finally quit completely.

Unlike other sports or hobbies where performance-enhancing drugs can be taken to 'cheat' a way to athletic excellence, when it comes to stretching it is simply a case of good old-fashioned hard work combined with time and perseverance that will win through.

Everyone has it within themselves to improve and increase their flexibility and stretching. Some will find it easier than others and the older you are when you start, the more work you will have to put in. However, if you would like to achieve good flexibility and an improved kicking ability, it is certainly worth the effort involved. Just be aware that, despite what others may have you believe, there is no substitute for dedication.

Stretching out the Hamstrings

From a standing position with your feet together, bend forwards from the waist as low as you can go. If you are new to stretching, your first target with this particular stretch is to try and touch your toes (Fig 155). If you are able to touch your toes, your next stage is to try and touch the floor. If you are able to touch the floor, then try to place your palms flat on the floor (156) and if you can do that, then try to get the backs of your hands on the floor (Fig 157). Hold the stretch at your lowest position for a count of 10 seconds.

From the same position reach down your legs and grab hold of your ankles. If you are unable to grab your ankles at this stage, try to grab hold of your legs as low as possible. As you need to anchor on to something for leverage for the next stretch,

sometimes simply grabbing the trousers will do the same job. From here pull your body down, attempting to get your chest as close to your legs as possible (Fig 158). Hold the stretch for a count of 10 seconds.

From here, sit on the floor and place your left leg out straight while tucking your right leg into the groin. Reach forward taking hold of the left foot with your left hand and support the left knee with your right hand to prevent it rising off the

Fig 155 (top left) Lean forwards and try to touch your toes.

Fig 156 (top right) Place your hands flat on the floor.

Fig 157 (bottom left) Place the back of your hands on the floor.

Fig 158 (bottom left) Grab your ankles and pull your body down.

Fig 159 Support your knee and lift your foot off the floor.

Fig 160 Pull your chest down to your leg.

floor. Then lift your left foot off the floor as high as you can (Fig 159). Hold the stretch for a count of 10 seconds. This stretch will also work the calf muscle.

Next, reach as far down the leg as you can and try to grab hold of either the foot or the ankle with both hands. Using this anchor as a lever, pull your chest down to your outstretched leg and attempt to get the chest (as opposed to the head, as this is a common cheat when performing this type of stretch) to lie flat against the leg (Fig 160). Hold for 10 seconds and then repeat the previous two stretching drills on your other side.

Now place both legs out together and, reaching forwards, try to grab your feet with both hands. If you can, lift both feet off the floor and hold for a count of 10 seconds (Fig 161).

From here, grab hold of your ankles with both hands and, using this grip as leverage, pull your chest (not your head) down to your outstretched legs for a count of 10 seconds (Fig 162).

To complete the hamstring stretch, finish with a stretching exercise known as the hurdling stretch. It is slightly more advanced but gives a good overall finish to the stretching in this particular area. Sit on the floor and place your left leg out in front of you. Curl the right leg round as far as you can and ensure you are sitting flat on the floor and not on your foot. This in itself involves a good level of flexibility (Fig 163). Now drop your body down to your forward leg, attempting to get your chest (not your head) as close to your leg as possible (Fig 164). Hold the stretch for a count of 10 seconds.

Fig 161 Lift both feet off the floor.

Fig 162 Pull your chest down to both legs.

From here, twist the body round to the rear leg and try to get your head as close to your knee as possible (Fig 165). Hold the stretch for a count of 10 seconds and then repeat the whole stretch again on the other side.

Fig 163 Sit in a hurdling position.

Fig 164 Pull your chest down to your forward leg.

Fig 165 Pull your head down to your rear leg.

Inner-Thigh Stretch

From an upright position (Fig 166), bend your legs and bring your fingertips in to the centre (Fig 167). Extend your left leg so that the left foot is on the heel and the right foot is on the ball. Take your

Fig 166 (left) From an upright position.

Fig 167 (below) Bend your knees.

Fig 168 (bottom) Place your left leg out to the side, resting on the heel.

57

right elbow and push your right knee out further and then place the hands firmly on the floor to stabilize yourself (Fig 168). At this point you should start to feel the stretch on the inner thighs; if you feel nothing, try sliding your left leg out slightly to the side. Hold for a count of 10 seconds and then repeat on the other side.

From the last position, take your body back over to the other side and this time ensure that both feet are kept flat on the floor (Fig 169). Push out once again with the elbow on the bent-leg side to increase the stretch and try to sink down low in the centre. Hold for a count of 10 seconds and then repeat on the other side.

Fig 169 Place your right leg out to the side resting on the flat of your foot.

Butterfly Stretch

This stretch is a good one for increasing flexibility in the adductor muscles in the hips, which is crucial when performing kicks of a high level. Aptly named the butterfly stretch due to the position of the legs while performing it, it also lends itself very nicely to the start position for the development of the side or box splits. From a seated position, grasping your right foot with your right hand and your left foot with your left hand, place your elbows on to your legs as shown and gently push down, bringing your legs as close to the floor as you can (Figs 170 to 171). If you can get your

legs to touch the floor then try leaning forwards and placing your head on the floor to take the stretch even further (Fig 172). Hold the stretch for a count of 10 seconds.

Fig 170 Bring your heels in to the body.

Fig 171 Push your legs to the floor, using your elbows.

Fig 172 Bring your head to the floor.

Developing the Box- or Side-Split Stretch

The box- or side-split stretch is probably the most important when it comes to kicking as it requires the legs to move in a way that is similar to the action used in the vast majority of kicks. Therefore, if you find yourself limited on time, or you are simply looking to focus more on a particular stretch, the following sequence of stretching drills is probably the best one to follow.

From an upright position with your feet just slightly wider than shoulder width (Fig 173), bend from the waist, aiming to place your hands on the floor (Fig 174). If you find that you can comfortably achieve this first position, bend lower and try placing your forearms and elbows on the floor (Fig 175). Hold this stretch for a count of 10 seconds.

Fig 175 Bring your elbows to the floor.

Fig 176 Grab your ankles and pull your body through your legs.

Fig 173 Stand with your legs double shoulder width.

Fig 174 Bring your hands to the centre.

Fig 177 Pull yourself down to your left leg.

59

From here, take hold of your ankles and pull your body through the centre of your legs as if you were trying to look up at the ceiling (Fig 176). Hold for a count of 10 seconds. Reach across to your left side and, if you can, take hold of your left foot with your right hand (if not then simply take hold of your leg at a point comfortable to you) and your leg with your left hand, and gently pull your body down towards your left leg (Fig 177). Be sure to keep your left leg locked out as the temptation here is to bend the knee to make the stretch easier. Hold for a count of 10 seconds and then repeat the same stretch on the other side.

From the last position, place your hands flat on the floor to support your body weight and, keeping your hips on the centre line, slide your legs out as far as they will comfortably go (Fig 178 to 179). Once you have found your maximum position for the start of this stretch, walk forwards with your hands, keeping the feet where they are so that you cross over the centre line (Fig 180), and bring the chest down to the floor as if performing a push-up (Fig 181).

Keep your body as low to the floor as you can and slowly push backwards using your hands so that you come up on to the backs of your heels

Fig 178 Support your body weight on your hands.

Fig 179 Slide your legs out wide.

Fig 180 Take a step forwards with your hands.

Fig 181 Bring your chest to the floor.

Fig 182 Stay low and push yourself backwards.

Fig 183 Come up on to your heels.

Fig 184 Bring your hands underneath your legs.

Fig 185 Return to the start position and repeat the exercise.

(Fig 182 to 183). From here, walk your hands underneath your legs (be careful not to lose your balance here and fall backwards) and bring your hips behind the centre line (Fig 184). Then return to your start position (Fig 185) and repeat the routine again a total of three times. The process of bringing your hips forwards and backwards in both a low position and a raised position will help to take the ligaments through their full range of motion, which in turn helps to increase their flexibility in all the ranges that are similar to those experienced when kicking.

Once you have completed the previous stretch, try gently lowering yourself down into a seated position (Fig 186). Alternatively, if you need to, have a walk around to reduce any stiffness you might have, and then sit down and open your legs as wide as you can in order to continue the next stretch where you left off.

With your legs in their widest position, reach over to your left leg and, by taking hold of your foot, ankle, leg or trouser (whatever you can comfortably reach), pull your chest down as close to your leg as you can and hold for a count

Fig 186 Sit with your legs wide.

Fig 187 Bring your chest down to your left leg.

Fig 188 Bring your chest to the centre.

Fig 189 Place your arms out to the side.

of 10 seconds (Fig 187). Repeat on the other side.

Finally, and to complete the stretching routine for the development of the side-split stretch, using your hands to support you, walk your body down to the ground, aiming to bring the chest as close to the floor as possible (Fig 188). If you can do this then place your arms out to the side and relax into the stretch for a count of 10 seconds (Fig 189).

Developing the Front-Split Stretch

This final stretch will greatly assist you when performing forward-moving kicks (as opposed to side-moving and circular kicks), such as the front kick and the axe kick. After this stretch you should

be fully ready to train every kick in every possible position, secure in the knowledge that you have correctly warmed yourself up and stretched out the main areas of the body that you will need to perform competently all of the kicks contained within a kickboxing syllabus.

From an upright position (hands on hips), step forward with your left leg as if performing a mini lunge (Fig 190). Hold the stretch for a count of 10 seconds. Then, working the stretch on the same side, straighten out the forward leg, locking the knee joint and, by taking hold of the ankle (or the lowest point you can comfortably manage), gently pull yourself down aiming to touch your chest to your leg (Fig 191). Hold the stretch for 10 seconds.

Fig 190 (top left) Step forwards as if performing a lunge.

Fig 191 (above) Bring your chest down to your lead leg.

Fig 192 (top right) Slide your rear leg out and place your hands on the floor.

Fig 193 Front-on view.

Fig 194 (centre right) Slide your lead leg out into a front split.

Fig 195 (right) Bring your chest down to your lead leg.

From here, bring the left hand underneath the left leg and, placing both hands on the floor for support, slide the right leg back until you begin to feel the stretch working (Fig 192). Hold for 10 seconds. Fig 193 shows the same stretch from a different angle so you can clearly see where to position the hands for maximum support. From here bring your left hand back out, and slide your front foot forwards, bringing the legs into a front-split stretch (Fig 194). Hold for 10 seconds.

Finally, reach as far down the left leg as you can and, taking hold of the ankle (or your lowest point), gently pull your body down aiming to place your chest on your leg (Fig 195). Repeat the whole routine on the other side.

Final Stretch

To complete your stretching routine, balance yourself on one leg and take hold of the ankle (not the foot) of your other leg, as shown. Ensure you keep your knees together and not sticking out to the side and push your hip forwards to increase the stretch (Fig 196). Hold for a count of 10 seconds and then repeat on your other side.

If you find your balance needs a little help here, either place your opposite arm out to the side and/or focus on a spot on the floor or wall in front of you. Alternatively, simply use a wall or other sturdy object as support but do not rely on this long term as the aim is also to develop your balance.

If you are working with a training partner at this point, you can both work this last stretch together by facing each other and placing your opposite hands to each other on each other's shoulders.

Fig 196 Grab your shin and pull the leg up behind.

7 Defence Against Punches

There are various ways a kickboxer can defend himself against a punch. In most kickboxing programmes there are six basic punches: the lead jab, rear cross, lead hook, rear hook, lead uppercut and rear uppercut. Some styles of kickboxing will also include the backfist strike, the spinning backfist strike and the elbow strike (lead and rear).

Other art forms outside of kickboxing may include slight variations of the straight, circular and rising attacks. Although the basic hand techniques only will be covered here (almost every stand-up art features a jab, cross, hook and uppercut attack of some description), if your style of kickboxing (or martial art) incorporates any other techniques, you can adapt the advice to use the most appropriate defence for the attacking angle of each technique.

My book *Kickboxing: From Beginner to Black Belt* (The Crowood Press, 2008) covers all the technical aspects of kickboxing, including stances, punching techniques and kicking techniques, and these do not need to be explained again here. If you are entering into the world of sparring, the assumption is that your technical ability and basic foundations are good enough to support what you are about to do. However, regardless of the level that you have attained, it is important to look at the three basic stances that you will use throughout this book, with a brief description of how the guard works while in each stance.

Your guard is quite simply your defence. It is the barrier between the attack and the connection that will undoubtedly decide whether the technique finds its mark or whether it is absorbed. If your guard is good, your opponent has a harder job of hitting you. On the other hand, if your guard is poor, you will have a harder job of defending each attack.

Ultimately it is better not to get hit at all and to this end you will use movement and evasion (*see* below). However, when movement and evasion are not possible, you need to ensure that you can actually defend the attack. Try not to think of your arms as mere blocking tools – in the style of the stars of many of the martial art movies that grace our screens – but think of them instead more as shields that you use to absorb the impact of an attack.

In kickboxing the attacks can be fast and furious. When performed by a competent kickboxing opponent, they more commonly consist of combinations containing multiple techniques instead of single attacks (as in other art forms). For this reason, bringing the arms away from the head and/or body – for example, to reach out and block a punch or kick, using the forearms as in the case of a rising-style block (defence against a punch, for example) or a descending-style block (defence against a kick, for example) – might not be the best use of your defences in this environment. A skilled opponent may take advantage of this to initiate a dummy attack, which you reach out to defend against, thus giving him an opportunity to immediately switch his attack in order to target the gap you have just left (more on this style of attack later).

You also need to consider that the guard is ever-changing. That is not to say that it morphs into something completely different, but that it will (or rather it should) change depending on the range you are in and the techniques that are being thrown. Anyone who tells you that the guard remains the same throughout the fight might not be giving you the best advice, as the defence against a punch to the head is probably not going to be the same as the defence against a kick to the body.

The Three Basic Stances

The following are the basic stances you will adopt when sparring, coupled with the three possible ways of holding your guard. These stances, along with the guard, will change many times throughout the fight, so try out each one to see how it feels and transition between stances using your footwork to find out how you change from one stance to the next as efficiently as possible.

The Front-On Stance

This is your most basic stance and might be adopted when punching or when being punched. The legs are around shoulder-width apart with weight distribution around 50/50 on the front and rear leg. The rear knee is turned slightly in and the rear foot is turned on to the ball.

The shoulders are slightly shrugged to reduce the possibility of whiplash if a strong straight attack lands to the head, and the rear hand is placed on the side of the chin with the rear elbow held tight against the body. The lead hand is held directly in line with the centre of the body. As with the rear hand, it is kept relaxed in order to move quickly between an attack to the head or body, or alternatively to initiate an attack as fast as possible. Tension reduces the speed of movement and ideally should be present only at the point of impact (Fig 197).

The Angled Stance

This universal stance allows for fast movement and access to all angles of attack, particularly with the kicks. It also slightly reduces the targets available to your opponent and the weight distribution here means that for the majority of the time the kicks are primed and ready to fire.

If you imagine a line running along the floor, you ideally need to position the heel of your rear foot and the ball of your lead foot on that line. The weight distribution should be around 70/30, with 70 per cent of your body weight on your rear leg. This will allow you to lift the lead leg off the floor quickly without the need to step up with the rear leg and, with a hop step, allows you rapidly to perform lead-leg kicks, for both attack and defence very quickly; a lead-leg side kick works well to stop a blitz attack in this position.

The rear hand is held in the same way as for the previous stance but the lead hand is now held in a slightly different way. Keep the lead elbow in tight

Fig 197 Front-on fighting stance.

Fig 198 Angled fighting stance.

to the body, being careful not to expose the area to the left of the arm; the lead hand should reside around the mid-section. Although there appears to be a slight gap in the defences here, your left arm can now pivot, rather like a windscreen wiper (in other words, up and down), and, in conjunction with the forward and backward movement of the rear arm, this helps to cover the gap nicely (more on this later) (Fig 198).

The Side-On Stance

The side-on stance is a great one to securely limit the target areas available to your opponent, but it does tend to take away the use of the rear hand slightly. For lead-leg attacks such as the side kick it is an excellent stance from which to work and, as you might expect, the rear-leg spinning kicks are much faster when used with this stance.

Using the same imaginary line as before, place both heels on the same line and again distribute the weight around 70/30. Keep the rear hand on the chin and the elbow into the body and shrug the lead shoulder slightly to add additional protection for

Fig 199 Side-on fighting stance.

the chin. Your lead arm and hand are held in much the same position as before, allowing the same windscreen-wiper movement to cover any gaps that might appear in your defence (Fig 199).

With all three stances you need to stay as light on your feet as possible and this is done by keeping most of your weight on the balls of your feet. Even in the warm-up you should stay up on the balls of your feet when bouncing from foot to foot, jogging and skipping. This is to get you used to moving around in this way when sparring, to stop you getting flat-footed and to allow you to move and switch position and attack, evade and defend as quickly as possible.

You will also move between stances throughout your fight and the guard will change accordingly. In the early stages of sparring this will need to be more as a result of conscious thought, however, as you become more experienced, your actions and reactions will become more subconscious and therefore a lot faster.

Basic Defence

Your basic defence against a punch will include the following:

- cover – using the arms to cover the area of attack;
- parry – using the hand to knock the attack off target;
- slip – moving the head to the side and out of the way of the punch;
- lean back – moving the head back and out of the way of the punch;
- circular evasion – moving the body from left to right or right to left;
- drop evasion – dropping the body underneath the attack;
- circular evasion – moving the body forwards or backwards;
- step back – moving the whole body backwards.

Covers

The cover is used by placing the arms in the way of the attack to prevent the attack from hitting the head or the body. The thought process is that the arms can take a lot more punishment than the head and the body can, so when the attacks are likely to be fast and multiple it is easier simply to use the arms as a shield and allow the attacks to land here instead. You will use the cover differently depending on how you are attacked, as follows.

Cover Against a Straight Punch to the Head

This will provide cover against straight punches, including jabs, crosses and so on, to the head.

Face your partner in a front-on stance with a front-on defence. As the punch comes in, raise your guard up in front of your face so the hands rest on the front of the head and the forearms take the blow. Slightly lean into the punch to help absorb it and be sure you can still see through the gap created by your forearms, so that you can defend any further attacks. The hands are positioned on the head to strengthen the attack; holding them in front of you will simply result in the force of the attack driving your own hands into your face (Fig 200).

Cover Against a Circular Attack to the Head

This will provide cover against hooks, elbows, backfists, spinning backfists and so on.

Fig 200 Defence against a straight punch.

Face your partner in a front-on stance as before. As the punch comes in, raise your defending arm straight up and position your hand at the rear of your neck. This will ensure the back of the head is

Fig 201 Defence against a circular punch.

Fig 202 Alternate defence against a circular punch.

covered should the attack swing out wide. It will also ensure there is very little gap between your forearm and your bicep where a punch can sometimes slip in. The blow is now absorbed on the side of the arm with the body facing forwards (Fig 201).

The alternative to this is to use a double forearm cover much like the one used for the straight attack. As the circular attack comes in, bring your guard up as before and turn the body into the attack. As you do, be sure not to take your eyes off your opponent. The temptation is to look at the punch, which of course means that you will not see a second attack coming (Fig 202).

Cover Against an Ascending Attack to the Head
This will provide cover against uppercuts, elbows, and so on.

This time, your opponent attacks with a rising attack such as an uppercut. Bring your arms together as with the first drill but, instead of bringing them high as before, lower them slightly in order to absorb the energy of the punch as it travels up the body. Make sure you can see through the natural gap created by the forearms (Fig 203).

Cover Against a Straight Attack to the Body
This will provide cover against jabs, crosses and so on, to the body.

Fig 203 Defence against an uppercut.

Fig 204 Defence against a mid-line straight punch.

As the punch comes in, bring your arms together as before but this time crunch the body slightly. This additional move ensures that the forearms cover the whole of the body, leaving no gaps. The hands are slightly lower than before, so that you can still see over the top of the gloves. If you try to place the hands on top of the head for this defence, the movement will cause the head to face down towards the floor and in turn take your eyes off your opponent (Fig 204).

Positioning the Eyes

A word on where to look. It is important that you never take your eyes off your opponent. Most people make the mistake of focusing on the attack, but if you do this, it is more likely that you will miss the second attack that follows. In reality, if you have blocked it, you already know where the first attack is, so looking at it is unnecessary.

When sparring it is important to keep your eyes positioned at such a level that you can clearly see any movement outside of the main field of your peripheral vision. Focusing around the chest area of your opponent, for example, should also ensure that you see attacks from the lead and rear hand and leg with equal effect. Focusing solely on that kick, however, means that it will be very difficult for you to also see that punch.

Fig 205 Defence against a mid-line circular punch.

Fig 206 Defence against a mid-line uppercut.

Cover Against a Circular Attack to the Body
This time, as the punch (a hook, elbow, backfist and so on) comes in, pull the elbow of the defending arm in tight towards the body. To make sure

that you are not leaving any gaps exposed try touching the elbow to the hip. Crunching the body to the side will help you achieve this. As before, bring the hand up to the head ensuring the chin is covered and, just for good measure, ensure the hand of your opposite arm is covering the other side of your chin (Fig 205).

Cover Against an Ascending Attack to the Body
As the punch (uppercut, elbow, and so on) comes in, drop the arms slightly so that the forearms meet the punch before it lands. Bring the hands in close to the face, ensuring that you can clearly see over the top of the gloves and slightly drop the body weight on to the punch to help absorb the energy of the blow (Fig 206).

Parries
A parry simply involves striking the attack in order to knock it off its target line. There is not a huge element of force required for this to be an effective move, however, it does rely on good timing. If you are too late, the attack will land; if you parry too soon, you will miss it. There are several variations of the parry, but the focus here is on a simple straight-line one, as this does not require you to move the hand too far away from the body and consequently ensures that you will still be able to return your guard quickly to a safe position.

Lead Parry Against a Straight Punch
From your front-on stance, time your parry so that, as your opponent's punch extends, your lead hand strikes his rear hand and knocks it off its target line. If you work this from a front-on guard there is actually little movement required for this highly effective defence to work. Be sure to keep your chin tucked safely behind your lead shoulder and keep your head low, just in case you miss your timing. The worst that will then happen is that the punch will hit the shoulder or bounce off the forehead, which is better than receiving it on the chin or temple (Fig 207).

Rear-Hand Parry Against a Straight Punch
As your opponent throws his straight punch (in this case a cross), bring your rear hand across the

Fig 207 Lead-hand inside parry.

Fig 208 Lead-hand outside parry.

front of your face just prior to the attack landing. If you time it right, this should be enough to knock his attack off target. As you perform this parry, do not move the whole arm; instead, as

The Knockout

There are three main knockout points on the head of which the kickboxer needs to be aware:

- the chin;
- the temple;
- the back of the head.

Taking a direct hit on any of these areas is not only likely to cause a knockout, but can also be quite dangerous, resulting in concussion or worse. You need to ensure that you protect these areas at all times. A knockout blow is thought to occur when the brain experiences some kind of trauma. A powerful blow to one of these areas can cause the head to move with such speed and force that the brain, which sits floating in cerebral fluid, can recoil inside, striking the back, side or front of the skull. This impact can cause trauma, which in turn temporarily short-circuits the nervous system causing the blackout effect commonly associated with a knockout.

described earlier, use the rear arm like a windscreen wiper, moving it slightly forward of the chin (where it should be resting) and pivoting it from the elbow joint. Use this 'wiping' motion to strike the attacking limb either with an open or closed palm, knocking it off its line of travel (Fig 208).

Lead-Hand Parry Against a Circular Attack
As your opponent throws his circular attack, bring your rear hand down so the rear elbow is high and the chin is tucked away safely behind the shoulder. At the same time, bring the lead hand in front of the face and stop the punch dead; for good measure, hide the head behind the hand you use to parry, the rear elbow and the rear shoulder. This defence will not knock the technique off its line of target but instead is used to stop the attack in its tracks before it finds its mark (Fig 209).

Rear-Hand Parry Against a Circular Attack
As the opponent switches his attack to follow with the rear hook, transfer your body over to the opposite side and switch the hand positions so your rear hand now meets the attack and your chin is tucked safely away behind the lead shoulder (Fig 210).

Fig 209 Lead-hand parry for circular punch.

Fig 210 Rear-hand outside parry.

Fig 211 Parry against an ascending attack.

Fig 212 Alternative parry against an ascending attack.

Rear-Hand Parry Against an Ascending Attack
As the attack travels upwards either towards the head or the body, bring your lead hand up so that it sits tightly on the chin, with the elbow tucked in close to the body. At the same time bring the rear hand in a downward motion, stopping the attacking punch in its tracks. To add extra energy to this parry step back slightly with your lead leg and as you do so tuck the chin behind the rear shoulder to protect it against the possibility of a lead hook from your opponent. Should that hook come, your left hand is of course primed and ready to parry it as before (Fig 211).

Lead-Hand Parry Against an Ascending Attack
As the attack travels up the body, bring your rear hand slightly forward of your face just in case a lead-hand straight punch follows, and at the same time drive the lead hand down on to the attack, stopping it from reaching its mark (Fig 212).

Slipping a Punch
'Slipping a punch' is a term commonly used when leaning out of the way of an attack. The most popular movement when slipping a punch is a sideways one, either to the left or to the right, and this method of defence is most effective against a straight punch.

Slipping a Jab
Timing is obviously key with this defence so you need to watch your opponent closely and spot any tell-tale signs that they are about to punch. Most inexperienced fighters will telegraph their intentions so, as soon as you see the straight punch begin, simply lean your head slightly to the side to avoid the punch landing. Be careful of moving the head back on to the same spot and instead use your footwork or your body movement to change your position (Fig 213).

Slipping a Cross
As with the previous drill, the cross should be somewhat easier to spot as it has further to travel.

Fig 213 Slip a punch – right.

Tell-Tale Signs

When a fighter telegraphs a technique they generally make some additional pre-strike movement that an experienced fighter will be able to pick up on and use to their advantage. Telegraphing a kick for example might involve a simple step up with the back foot or a slight drop of the guard prior to kicking. Typical telegraphs for a punch usually involve pulling back the attacking arm or a roll of the shoulder on the punching side.

There are many more tell-tale signs that give away the fact that your opponent is about to attack if you look for them. Your job as a fighter is to spot them as they happen, determine from that particular movement which attack is most likely to follow, and be ready for it as it happens. It is about being proactive instead of reactive. For example, a step up probably means a kick is on its way. If the opponent is front-on as they step it is more likely to be a front-on attack such as a front kick. If they start to swing their leg as they step, then it may be possibly an axe kick that is coming. This simple but effective principle will make a big difference between you getting hit from an attack and knowing what is coming and defending it when it happens.

Whether it is a jab or a cross, the principle is still the same. As the punch comes into range, move the head off the target line by slipping it either to the left or the right. Whether you move left or right is a decision you need to make instantaneously with as little conscious thought as possible (the longer you spend thinking about it, the less time you have to move and the more likely it is to land). Generally, if you happen to have most of your body weight to the right it would be quicker to move the head to the right, and vice versa. The other consideration is that, if your opponent jabs while in a left lead, for example, you might stand a greater chance of a successful counter if you attack to his inside, particularly if his defence is weak (Fig 214); in this case, you would be better off moving to your left.

Lean-Back Slip

It is also possible to slip a punch by using a technique known as the 'lean-back'. Quite simply, as the punch comes in, you keep your feet positioned where they are and lean back slightly so that the

Fig 215 Lean-back evasion against a straight punch.

Fig 214 Slip a punch – left.

Fig 216 Lean-back evasion against an ascending attack.

74

attack falls short of the head. This simple move works well against all attacks regardless of whether they are straight, circular or ascending. Fig 215 shows the lean-back slip working against a jab and Fig 216 shows the same technique working against an uppercut.

Evading a Punch

Evading a punch, also known as 'roll and recover', is probably one of the most skilful forms of defence you can use. The speed, timing and body mechanics all come into play together and need to work in harmony with one another in order for the defence to work. It also allows for an excellent counter-strike if done properly (more about this later).

When evading a punch in this way, particularly for the kickboxer, you are at risk of a kick or, depending on the art you study, a knee strike,

should your speed and timing not be up to scratch. If you are a bit slower than your opponent, then down low and in perfect range for a knee is probably the last place you want to be. The other thing to be aware of is that there is a correct and an incorrect way to roll and if you get this wrong, you could very well end up rolling into the attack.

Evading a Lead Circular Attack

As your opponent starts his attack, drop down low to the inside of the punch, circling your body to your left, and keep your guard tight, just in case (left hand on the chin, left elbow into the body, right shoulder covering the right side of the chin, right arm covering the body). As the punch comes over the top of your head, roll your body underneath it and come back up to your fighting stance. Figs 217 and 218 show the correct way to roll when dealing with a lead circular attack of this nature.

Fig 217 Start of a circular evasion against a lead hook.

Fig 218 Finish position for circular evasion.

Fig 219 Start of a circular evasion against a rear hook.

Fig 220 Finish position for circular evasion.

Evading a Rear Circular Attack

As the rear punch comes in, transfer your weight on to your rear leg and drop the body underneath the punch, again keeping the guard tight (right hand on the chin, right elbow into the body, left shoulder covering the left side of the chin, left arm protecting the body). As the punch passes overhead, twist the body underneath it and come back up into your fighting stance. Figs 219 and 220 show the correct way to roll when dealing with a rear circular attack such as a rear hooking punch.

Notice on both examples how the feet move to power the body through the various stages of the roll. It is not just a case of keeping the feet static and bending the body as this will bring the head too close to the lower weapons of your opponent and in turn expose the back of the head. Instead, and to ensure the movement works correctly, you need to bend from the knees, keep your head in line with (or behind) your forward knee, and use your legs to move the body from left to right or right to left, depending on which way you are rolling.

Also, observe how the guard changes as you transition from one side to the other. This is done to ensure that the hand nearest to your opponent is free to counter-punch and that no part of the chin is left exposed as you roll.

Drop Evasion

This style of defence works really well against a straight punch and is slightly different in its approach from the last two. It is also a great one to use against an opponent who tends to throw a lot of single punches, particularly straight ones, although it will still work against the circular attacks and simply gives you another option when confronted with these types of punch.

As your opponent throws his punch (in this case a jab), simply drop your body down so the punch goes over the top of your head and at the same time exposes their mid-section. As with all the defences

Fig 221 Drop evasion.

Fig 222 Face your opponent.

so far, be sure to keep your chin covered and make sure you can see your opponent in case they follow up with a second attack (Fig 221).

The drop evasion defence is quite a fast one so once you get confident with it you can try baiting your opponent by lowering your guard slightly, encouraging them to jab to your head and giving you the opportunity to work your drop evasion along with a counter-punch. Obviously, you should train it with a sparring partner first before trying it in competition.

Step-Back Defence

This final defence needs a bit of confidence as well as practice to pull off as there is a risk of actually being caught by the attack if you do not get it right. Although you are covering yourself to a certain extent with this one, the defence works by moving out of range of the attack just enough so that it does not actually land. If you misjudge this, you stand a huge chance of getting hit, so be careful. This is not a defence you would really utilize

Fig 223 Step-back defence from a straight punch.

Fig 224 Step-back defence against a circular punch.

against an attack to the head, when you would look at using the lean-back. However, when you need to move quickly to avoid an attack to the body, it is certainly one to consider.

In a fighting stance (Fig 222), as your opponent throws his punch, shift your body weight on to your back foot, moving the body out of the way of the punch (Fig 223). This defence is effective because you are not actually moving your feet, so it is a very fast defence, and at the same time you are still close enough to your opponent to counter. Fig 224 shows the same defence working against a circular attack to the body.

8 Defence Against Kicks

The kick is an incredibly powerful weapon and, when delivered by a skilled opponent, can be quite devastating. It is several times more powerful than a punch. The other major advantage the kicker has over the puncher is distance. Distance, and successful control of it, is key to a fight and there are several ranges you need to consider when sparring.

The principles of defending against a kick are not dissimilar to those that relate to defending against a punch, but there are still some common mistakes that many fighters make. Following the principles described here will ensure that your defence against a kick is as effective as your defence against a punch.

Ranges in Sparring

- Out of range – this is the distance generally found at the start of any competitive fight, when both fighters are too far away to land anything. It can be drawn upon by utilizing good footwork and movement during the fight should one fighter need a few seconds to regain his composure, either because of fatigue or when attempting to recover from a successful blow from his opponent.
- Kicking range – this is the next range most commonly found in a fight, when the participants are just out of reach of punches but close enough for kicks. For the puncher it can be a difficult range at which to fight if his opponent is skilled with his kicks. The best way to deal with someone at this range is to move out of range completely and let the kicker wear himself down by chasing you. Alternatively, you can try to work around the kicks using speed and timing and reduce the gap between you so you are in the punching range.
- Punching range long – there are a number of ranges at which you can work with punches. In the long punching range, you can use straight punches such as the jab and cross. Because they travel in a straight line from your guard to full extension, they are excellent punches to use when the kicking range has been closed but you are still too far away to grab hold of your opponent. This range is probably the most versatile as you can move into close range or back into kicking range with relative ease.

- Punching range short – this is where the circular punches such as the hooks and uppercuts come in to play. These punches can be done over long range, but pulling off a long-range hook, for example, leads to a much greater risk of exposing the chin for a longer period of time. Generally this is the range at which you could comfortably grab hold of your opponent, so the punches will utilize the body mechanics more in order to do their job. The elbows and knee strikes will also come in to play.
- Upright grappling – depending on the type of sparring for which you train, you might find that you go no further than short-range punching. However, it does not end there. In the upright grappling range, commonly found in fighting arts such as Thai boxing, neck and body clinches come in to play. This also sets up the takedown, which takes the fight into the final stage – the ground.
- The ground – fighting at this range requires considerable experience of fighting on the floor. If you have little to no ground-fighting experience, having focused on stand-up fighting only, this area is best avoided in a fight. This area of fighting has become very popular recently with the MMA (mixed martial art) fighters, particularly those famous for fighting in a cage or octagon-style arena. It is worth familiarizing yourself with this fighting range, if for no other reason than simply knowing how to defend against it.

Covers

The power of a kick is several times more devastating than the power of a punch so, when defending against a kick in this way, be sure your guard is strong. As you receive the kick on the arms, block with the lower forearms and not the wrists. You may get away with using your wrists against a punch, although it is still not advisable. Receiving a full contact kick on this area could result in some serious damage so be sure your actual blocking area is correct.

Front-On Defence Against a Mid-Line Straight Kick

This type of defence works well against the straight kicks such as the front kick, side kick and spinning back kick, and so on. Just be sure you keep your arms tightly together so the kick does not slip through the gap in the middle, particularly when defending against a front kick.

From your front-on stance, as your opponent attacks, bring your arms together and your hands up to your head to form a shield. Shrug your shoulders slightly to reduce the risk of whiplash as the kick lands, and lean in to the kick to prevent yourself from being kicked backwards. This will also ensure you meet the energy of the kick with your energy to reduce the overall impact that the kick will have when it lands (Fig 225).

Front-On Defence Against a High-Line Straight Kick

The golden rule – using the lower forearms rather than the wrists, in order to reduce the risk of injury to the latter – goes out of the window slightly with this one. Because there is an inherent risk of exposing the body in attempting to use the forearms, as you would need to raise the arms quite high in order to defend against a head-height kick, the gloves would be used instead.

It is possible to use the forearms for this cover, however, it is also quite possible that anyone skilled enough to kick to the head in this way may be setting you up for a head and body double kick combination, so you need to keep as much of the body covered as possible as you defend against the head kick (Fig 226).

Fig 225 Front-on defence against a mid-line straight kick.

Fig 226 Front-on defence against a high-line straight kick.

Fig 227 Front-on defence against a high-line circular kick.

Front-On Defence Against a High-Line Circular Kick

This defence works well against the high-line circular kicks such as the round kick, hooking kicks, crescent kicks and spinning circular kicks. As the kick comes in, bring your blocking arm up high as if attempting to grab the back of your neck with your hand. This motion will close the gap between your forearm and bicep, ensuring that the kick does not slip through the gap you naturally create.

The other reason for attempting to block so deep is in case your opponent kicks round to the back of the head. Some hooking kicks are designed to attack this area so keep the back of the neck covered as well. Alternatively if your opponent uses the ball of the foot to attack with instead of the instep (in the case of a round kick), this striking tool is more likely to find its mark (Fig 227).

Front-On Defence Against a Mid-Line Circular Kick

By simply keeping your guard where it should be you will be able to deal with this kick with very

Fig 228 Front-on defence against a mid-line circular kick.

little effort. A common mistake that the inexperienced kicker will make is to simply kick the guard. This practice can be seen a great deal amongst most fighters in any stand-up art and all it does is tire them out (as you are still expending the same amount of energy as if you were kicking on target) and give their opponent a great opportunity to counter their kick (more on this later).

As the kick comes in, simply keep the guard in place and brace yourself for impact. As before, a slight lean in to the kick will help to absorb it and ensure you stand your ground ready for the next move (Fig 228).

Angled or Side-On Defence Against a Mid-Line Straight Kick

The principle of this defence works the same from either an angled stance or a side-on stance so it

Fig 229 Angled or side-on defence against a mid-line straight kick.

Fig 230 Angled or side-on defence against a high-line straight kick.

Fig 231 Angled or side-on defence against a mid-line circular kick to the inside.

Fig 232 Angled or side-on defence against a mid-line circular kick to the outside.

does not really matter which of these two you adopt. As the kick comes in, bring your arms in close, as if trying to touch your forearms together, to create a barrier. Tuck your chin behind your lead shoulder and keep your rear hand up high. Your lead hand will rest across your body, protecting the mid-line and the action of both arms coming together in this way doubles the strength of the defence and reduces the likelihood of the kick breaking through your guard. This type of defence is sometimes known among the point fighters as the universal block – aptly named, as it is a very effective defence against a lot of attacks (Fig 229).

Angled or Side-On Defence Against a High-Line Straight Kick

Using exactly the same method as before, tuck your chin behind your lead shoulder, as this is ultimately the target for which your opponent is aiming. Bring your lead arm across the body and either bring your rear arm forward to meet your lead hand (exactly as before), or keep the hand tight against the chin to add cover to the opposite side in case of a double kick (Fig 230).

Angled or Side-On Defence Against a Mid-Line Circular Kick to the Inside

This time the kick travels in a circular motion so, although the defence is very similar to the previous one, the emphasis is now on defending the side of the body as opposed to the front of the body. As you bring the arms together, turn slightly in towards the kick ensuring that the kick hits the double forearm barrier instead of the body (Fig 231).

Angled or Side-On Defence Against a Mid-Line Circular Kick to the Outside

This example should help you to understand fully how the body needs to move in order to block the kick successfully. As your opponent attacks to the outside of your body (in this case, using a lead hooking kick), bring your arms together and turn your body from the inside towards the outside so you block the kick with both arms, doubling the strength of the defence (Fig 232). The rear hand comes across to the other side of the chin in order to back up the lead arm and to ensure that you can twist out fully.

Fig 233 Angled or side-on defence against a high-line circular kick.

Angled or Side-On Defence Against a High-Line Circular Kick

This defence is different from the single-arm cover used for the front-on stance as it adopts the same principle as the previous drills and utilizes the double-forearm cover. Attempting to grab the back of the neck as for the front-on stance will leave the head dangerously exposed. For this reason, the rear hand is brought up slightly using the glove to absorb the kick and this is backed up by bringing the lead arm up but maintaining the fist-to-the-floor position. This will allow you to maintain a degree of cover to the body and ensure you can quickly move the guard should the opponent follow up with a kick to a different area. The most likely second attack is a side kick to the front of the body (Fig 233).

Fig 234 Front-on mid-line parry against a straight kick.

Fig 235 Front-on high-line parry against a straight kick.

Fig 236 Front-on high-line parry against a circular kick.

Fig 237 Front-on mid-line parry against a circular kick.

Parries

Parrying a kick requires a significant amount of skill and timing so, unless you are fighting a complete beginner, it should not be attempted before you have had many hours of practice. As with parrying a punch, the objective is to time your defence exactly so that, when the kick comes in, you can hit it with your palm and knock it off course. If your timing is not yet up to speed, you miss the kick by being either too early or too late, and the kick will find its mark.

Front-On Mid-Line Parry
Against a Straight Kick
Fig 234 shows a lead-hand parry against a lead-leg side kick. The rear hand is kept securely in position in case the opponent recovers and comes back with a hooking kick or similar. Ideally, when you parry a kick in this way, you are also attempting to use the energy of the movement to knock your partner off balance. They will not necessarily fall over, of course, but they will need to regain their balance before committing to a second attack, buying you enough time to counter.

Front-On High-Line Parry
Against a Straight Kick
The body of the defender is different in this parry from the previous one. As the straight kick (in this case, another side kick) travels towards its mark, the attack is parried in much the same way, except that the body slips to the side. This is done to keep the head off the centre line and is another way of avoiding the kick landing (Fig 235).

Front-On High-Line Parry
Against a Circular Kick
Rather than knocking the kick off its line, the parry in this instance is used to stop the kick dead in its tracks. As the circular kick comes in (in this case, an outside crescent kick), meet it with your opposite hand as before. Slip the head off the centre line just in case and keep your non-blocking arm around the mid-section for added defence (Fig 236).

Front-On Mid-Line Parry
Against a Circular Kick
In the same way as for the previous defences, time your parry so that, just before your opponent's kick reaches its mark, your hand is there to stop it (Fig 237).

Parry Using the Shoulder
This defence uses an area of the body that most would not consider using to parry an attack, however, with some practice, it is actually a really effective defending tool, particularly when used against an axe kick. When faced with an axe kick, most people will duck into the kick. In fact, one of the best forms of defence is to raise the lead shoulder, tucking the chin safely behind it, and, as the kick lands, twist the body inwards so the foot slides off. This manoeuvre takes some practice as well as some confidence to pull off but, if you can master it, it adds a very useful blocking tool to your fighting game (Fig 238).

Fig 238 Parry using the shoulder.

Fig 239 Face your opponent.

Fig 240 Step back with your lead leg.

Fig 241 Complete the step-back evasion.

Evasions

The best scenario is where you can hit without being hit, and evasions help you avoid being hit at all. Of course, it is near-impossible to spar or fight competitively without something landing – even world-class fighters get hit – but a good under-standing of the evasion will reduce the amount of impact your body takes, which of course can only be a good thing.

Shuffle Step-Back Evasion
Against a Mid-Line Straight Kick

Square off against your opponent (Fig 239). As they chamber the leg in readiness for the kick, bring your lead leg back towards your rear leg (Fig 240). As they start to extend the kick, complete the evasion by stepping back with your rear leg and out of the way (Fig 241). The movement needs to be quick and explosive to ensure you are far enough away from the kick to avoid it completely. It needs to be even more dynamic if your opponent steps in with the kick as a slight movement backwards probably will not be enough.

Fig 242 Face your opponent.

Fig 243 Step back with your lead leg.

Fig 244 Complete the evasion.

Shuffle Step-Back Evasion Against a Mid-Line Circular Kick

Even with the kick travelling in a different direction, the evasion remains the same, making this one of the easiest defences to understand (although understanding it and doing it are two different things). Face your opponent as before (Fig 242). As they chamber their leg, step back with your lead leg (Fig 243) and, as they execute the kick, complete the shuffle step back to evade the attack (Fig 244). Again, this needs to be a swift, dynamic movement. Move back out of the way as soon as you are aware of what is coming. Your ability to read and react will make the difference between getting out of the way of an attack or getting hit by it.

Shuffle Step-Back Evasion Against a High-Line Circular Kick

As you face your opponent, watch for some tell-tale sign that they are about to attack. Most inexperienced fighters will telegraph

Fig 245 Face your opponent.

Fig 246 Bring your lead leg back.

Fig 247 Shuffle-step back.

their techniques, so look out for this (Fig 245). As you see them move into position for the high-line kick bring your lead leg back to your rear leg and shuffle-step back with your rear leg to avoid the kick (Figs 246 and 247).

Shuffle Step-Back Evasion Against a High-Line Descending Kick

Most fighters faced with an axe kick will duck into the kick, but it is better to defend against it using the shoulder to parry with. The shuffle-step evasion works just as well and is another alternative to defending against a descending kick such as an axe kick, if you have the area and the time to react. From your fighting stance (Fig 248), step back with your lead leg as soon as you see the kick starting to rise (Fig 249). At the same time and as one explosive movement, shuffle-step back with your rear leg taking you safely out of range of the kick (Fig 250).

Fig 248 Face your opponent.

Fig 249 Step back with your lead leg.

Fig 250 Shuffle-step back.

Lean-Back Defence Against a High-Line Straight Kick

The lean-back defences involve a simple body movement to evade the kick. The simplicity of the movement means it is a lot faster to use. There is no need to step; instead, you simply lean out of the way and even if the kicker steps in deep in order to set up their kick, by simply keeping the guard in place, you're already set up to cover the kick with your lead arm, should it still actually hit you. This defence works the same whether your opponent kicks mid or high level.

From your fighting stance (Fig 251), keeping the feet where they are, simply transfer your body weight on to your rear leg and lean back out of the way of the kick (Fig 252).

Lean-Back Defence Against a High-Line Circular Kick

As the kick steps in, transfer your weight on to your rear foot and simply lean back out of the way so the kick passes in front of you. Keep the guard in place just in case your opponent decides to follow up

Fig 251 Face your opponent.

Fig 252 Transfer your weight on to your back foot.

Fig 253 Face your opponent.

with a double kick and be prepared to use your footwork to move you further out of range should you need to (Figs 253 and 254). Again, this defence will work the same way against a mid-line kick, so you need to practise both variations.

Blocking an Attack

Blocking an attack is a common practice more widely seen among the traditional arts such as karate and taekwon-do. This type of defence works very well against a powerful, long-range single attack, such as a traditional reverse punch or roundhouse kick. It is also a very natural thing to do – this is clear from the way that anyone new to sparring reacts when a punch or a kick comes towards them. The body instinctively wants to block the attack before it can get close to the head

Fig 254 Lean back to avoid the attack.

Fig 255 Rising block against an axe kick.

or body, so instead of covering up as previously described, the natural thing to do is to stick out an arm in the hope that it connects with the attacker's limb and stops it this way.

This is all very well, as long as your opponent is not wise to it. It would be very easy to fake an initial attack in the hope that the beginner attempts to block it, thereby exposing a vital area.

Rising Block Defence Against an Axe Kick

As the kick comes in, bring your lead arm straight up in front of your head, attempting to connect with the kick before it lands (Fig 255). When performing this defence you will leave your mid line exposed and vulnerable (if your opponent baits you with the axe kick, there is a possibility of a lead-leg side kick or reverse punch landing to the exposed area), so you must ensure that you bring

your rear arm slightly forward of your centre line (not visible in the photograph) so that you have at least created a barrier.

Rising Block Defence Against a Lead-Arm Attack

This defence can work against a lead jab or backfist strike; Fig 256 shows clearly where the rear hand needs to be positioned. This arm is primed and ready to fire out a cross or reverse punch to the opponent's exposed area, or alternatively defend against a second attack such as a round kick, front kick or even cross punch from the opponent.

Lead-Arm Inner Block Defence Against a Round Kick

You should have a good idea by now of how every technique can be blocked in this way. This final

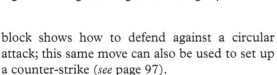

Fig 256 Rising block against a straight punch.

Fig 257 Inner-arm defence against a round kick.

block shows how to defend against a circular attack; this same move can also be used to set up a counter-strike (*see* page 97).

As your opponent commits to the attack, keep your guard in place and turn into the kick with your body, so that you block it using your forearm. You can bring the arm away from the body in order to block the kick (*see* Figs 255 and 256) but, wherever you can, you should try to keep the body as tightly covered as possible. In this way, you run less risk of exposing a target area that your opponent can hit with a second attack (Fig 257).

Absorbing the Attack

Absorbing the attack is not for the faint-hearted, as you will of course get hit. The difference is that you and not your opponent are in control of that hit. If you absorb the blow properly, the only area that should take it is the arm, which is used to block the vast majority of attacks, and can take much more punishment than the head or body can.

The idea behind absorbing an attack is to catch the opponent off guard; if it is done correctly, it can be used to your advantage. Again, timing is vital. If you do not move in to absorb the attack at the correct moment, you might find yourself on the receiving end of a kick or punch travelling at full velocity as you move into it.

Step-In Defence Against a Mid-Line Circular Kick

This type of attack is a good one to start off with as it is relatively easy to defend against and therefore a step-in defence can be attempted with very little risk. From your fighting stance (Fig 258), as soon as you see your opponent step up to kick, keep your rear arm tight to the body and step forwards into the kick (Fig 259).

Your aim is to step in to your opponent, taking you into one of the punching ranges, and not to step into the kick. It just so happens that, by stepping in to your opponent in this way, the kick (or, rather, the knee in this case) will actually make

Fig 258 Face your opponent.

Fig 259 Step in to absorb the attack.

contact with your arm. This is acceptable because you have controlled it and, as your opponent is trying to regain his balance and stance, you can unload with your punches.

Step-In Defence Against a High-Line Circular Kick

The same line of defence works against a high-line circular kick such as a round kick or hooking kick. The only difference is that you keep your guard much higher, as your opponent will be looking to attack the head and his knee will be a lot higher at the start of the kick (Fig 260).

Step-In Defence Against an Axe Kick

This is another variation of defence that can be used against an axe kick. As your opponent steps up to begin his kick, step into the attack, putting yourself too close for the kick to land. If this is done correctly, you should be on the outside of your opponent making it very difficult for him to counter-attack your defence (Fig 261).

Fig 260 Step in to absorb the high-line attack.

Fig 261 Step in to absorb a descending attack.

Fig 262 Step in to absorb a side kick.

Fig 263 Face your opponent.

Fig 264 Step in to absorb a spinning kick.

Step-In Defence Against a Mid-Line Straight Kick

This demonstration uses a side kick, but the principle is the same against any straight kick. It works better if your opponent telegraphs the kick with a step-up. As soon as you see them step, move in to cover the distance, bringing yourself in too close for the kick to extend. At this point the energy created by your forward motion should put him off balance, giving you time to land a few counterattacks before he regains his composure (Fig 262).

Step-In Defence Against a Spinning Kick

This final demonstration shows how such a simple defence can work against every type of kick. As your opponent sets up the spin (Fig 263), time your entry correctly and step forwards into the kick so that you are too close for the technique to land (Fig 264). The beauty of this one is that it does not matter whether the spin is being used to set up a hook kick or a back kick; as soon as your opponent turns his back, you move in to work your defence.

Shin Blocks

The shin block completes the repertoire of defences against an attack. It is more commonly associated with the low-level kicking arts such as Thai boxing or certain styles of full-contact karate and kickboxing. It is an excellent defence against low-level kicks and works particularly well against circular attacks such as the round kick.

Low-level kicks are very difficult to defend against using the arms; in fact, it is very unlikely that you would even attempt to block one using your arm. Also, because of the damage they can do when used to attack the legs, you do not want to be taking too many of them. This is where the shin block comes in. The shin block is a very fast, responsive defence against a low- or even mid-line attack from a kick and, when used properly, can stop an attack of this nature from causing any serious damage to your legs or upper body.

Shin-Block Defence Against a Straight Kick

In this attack, your opponent is using a side kick to attack the leg. This kind of attack is not

Fig 265 Shin-block defence against a straight kick.

performed too often, particularly in the sport aspect of martial arts, but, as it could happen, you need to understand how to defend against it in this way. At the same time, if your flexibility allows, the shin could also be used to defend against a side kick (or other straight-leg attack) to the body. Just be careful that the power of the attack does not knock you over, particularly as you are now on only one leg (Fig 265). At the same time as defending with your shin, keep your guard tight and try to create a shield or barrier using your leg, elbow, forearm and hands.

Rear Shin-Block Defence Against a Round Kick

This is probably the more realistic way of attacking the leg and, when the sport allows, is also the favoured area to kick as it is faster and uses less energy than kicking to the head. It is also a great way to break an opponent down and many fights have been won through the use of low-level round kicks alone. It is not advisable simply to take these

Fig 266 Shin-block defence against a circular kick.

Fig 267 Lead shin-block defence.

kicks, regardless of how conditioned you believe your legs to be. Eventually, the kicks will break you down, leaving you unable to use the leg effectively for movement or attack. Thereafter, it will be only a matter of time before the inevitable happens.

It it very difficult to block these low-level attacks using just the arms. When faced with an attack of this nature, the most effective means of defence is again the shin block. The attack can come off either the lead or rear leg so you need to understand how to defend against both variations. It is also possible to defend using either shin, although this is more commonly determined by the stance you adopt when the attack comes in.

As your opponent kicks, simply bring your rear shin up and forwards in order to meet the attack straight on (Fig 266). The advantage of using the shin is that it can be quite quickly brought into play and you therefore stand a greater chance of actually defending this kind of attack. It is also a larger part of the body, which makes it more effective and easier to block with as there is more surface area to stop an attack.

Lead Shin-Block Defence Against a Round Kick

If you find yourself more on your back foot as the attack comes in, one alternative method of defence might be to use your lead shin instead. Realistically, you will probably have milliseconds within which to react when a kick is thrown – hardly enough time to readjust your stance, weight distribution and defence tactics. Instead, you will need to cover the attack using the nearest shield available and this will inevitably be your lead shin. Your objective with this is to bring the shin up and round almost as if you were trying to knee-strike your opponent in his shin. A slightly angled stance will help a great deal with the effectiveness of this defence. Again, you also need to ensure that you keep your guard tight, just in case you misjudge your opponent's intended striking area (Fig 267).

9 Counters Against Punches Using Punches

Defending an attack is all well and good, but it is of little use if you do not know what to do afterwards. It is quite possible (but unlikely) that you could stand and block every attack thrown at you without striking back, but this type of approach would certainly lose you the fight, one way or another.

Instead, you need to understand how to counter an attack as this is the more realistic approach to the fight. Quite often, a good counter-fighter (someone who purposefully waits to be attacked so that they can then defend or evade the attack and use timing to land a successful return strike on their opponent) will beat an out-and-out striker in competition. Having said that, you should not make the mistake of thinking that a counter-fighter will not take the lead sometimes and become a striker. Most fighters favour one style of fighting but the great fighter is someone who can switch between styles to adapt to their opponent throughout the fight.

There are a number of simple yet effective counter-strikes to some of the basic punches with which you are likely to be attacked. For ease of training, these counter-strikes are categorized here into sections, so you can start off training the techniques in the first section and, when competent with these, move on to the techniques in the next section, and so on.

Counter a Punch Using a Jab

The jab is a vital counter weapon. It is an incredibly fast attacking tool and is generally used to set up a knockout attack. Although the counter-attack is explained here as finishing at just one punch, you need to understand that, when you have your opponent on the back foot, so to speak, it would be inadvisable to leave it at just one attack. Instead,

you should always be looking at a second or third or fourth or fifth, and so on, as many fights are won when the opponent is stunned by an effective blow and is trying to recover. To allow your opponent the opportunity to recover would be wasting the advantage you have just gained for yourself and, more importantly, could cost you the fight.

All the defences described here are covered in Chapter 7.

Drill 1 – Cover and Counter

As your opponent jabs, defend using a double block (Fig 268). As he retracts his punch, follow

Fig 268 Defend a straight attack.

Fig 269 Counter with a straight attack.

Fig 270 Parry an attack.

Fig 271 Clear the attack.

Fig 272 Counter with a straight punch.

Fig 273 Slip a punch.

Fig 274 Counter with a jab.

straight back with a jab of your own (Fig 269). The success of this counter is based on speed and timing. As soon as you block the attack, immediately return it with a jab. If done correctly you should land your punch, even if your opponent is planning on a double-jab combo. Remember to keep your rear hand up and tuck the chin behind the lead shoulder as you punch.

Drill 2 – Parry and Counter

This time, as the punch comes in, parry it as previously explained, with your rear hand (Fig 270). Clear it out of the way with the same hand and bring your lead hand up and over the top (Fig 271) and, as you clear your rear hand, strike over the top of your arm keeping the opponent's lead hand trapped with your rear one (Fig 272). The effectiveness of this one is all down to the explosion. Although this cannot be shown clearly in the figures, the parry, clear and strike need to be done as fast as possible in order to increase the chances of your jab landing.

Drill 3 – Slip and Counter

As your opponent attacks, slip left, transferring your body weight on to your lead leg (Fig 273). Be sure to keep your chin tucked firmly behind your right shoulder (when in a left lead). At the same time as slipping the punch, counter with a jab to the head (Fig 274). Try to think of this as one movement (slip and jab together) as opposed to two movements (slip and then jab). A momentary pause between slipping the punch and then jabbing could buy your opponent a second in which to move.

Drill 4 – Speed Counter

This drill is very simple, but it can be very effective. Admittedly, it works better when facing a less experienced opponent as a more experienced fighter is less likely to make this common mistake. As you see your opponent telegraph his technique, use your explosive speed to beat him to the punch (Fig 275).

The opponent here has drawn his arm back slightly, probably in an attempt to draw up more

Fig 275 Explosive counter using a jab.

Fig 276 Counter an uppercut with a jab.

power. This is a common mistake, as it buys you a second with which to beat him to the mark. In order for this to work you need your jab to be primed and ready, almost waiting for him to make this mistake. Watch him throughout the early stages of the fight and, as soon as you spot the tell-tale signs that an attack is eminent, launch yours first. To help you understand how to prime your jab, try thinking of it as a coiled spring that you just release.

Drill 5 – Cover and Counter
This time your opponent steps in to uppercut the body. Keep your rear arm in tight to the body (this is where it should be anyway, so you should not have to do much), and bring it slightly forwards. At the same time as your opponent punches, send your jab out to the head (Fig 276).

Drill 6 – Drop and Counter
This time you are going to bait the attack from your opponent. You need to be very careful and make sure you are skilled enough at this level to see the attack coming. Practise this with several training partners at various speeds before attempting it for real.

From your fighting stance, slightly lower the guard on your lead hand in order to expose the head more. Keep the rear hand in place, but again slightly lower, so your opponent now has a clear view of your head (Fig 277). It is advisable to keep the head slightly back so that it is more over your back leg than the front, as this would put it too close to your opponent's jab. The idea is to give your opponent the impression that your head is open when in fact you are completely in control of the fact that it is not.

As soon as you see your opponent commit to his attack, drop down and jab to the body (Fig 278). It is more or less impossible for a fighter to cover this area once he has committed to a jab so, as long as you can get your head out of the way before his jab lands, you are almost 100 per cent likely to hit the target. As you drop, you put your head in the firing range of a round kick, so keep your guard tight and your head covered, just in case.

Fig 277 Bait your opponent.

Fig 278 Drop and counter.

Fig 279 Cover a body punch.

Fig 280 Counter with a straight punch.

Drill 7 – Counter to a Body Punch

When your opponent throws a cross punch to your body, bring your rear arm forwards to meet the attack and cover your body at the same time (Fig 279). In the same motion, throw out your jab, turning the body slightly in order to get the correct angle and punching over the top of your opponents arm, aiming for the temple or for their chin if it's exposed (Fig 280). This slight turning motion with the body will help you generate more power with your counter-punch and also move you out of the attacking line of your opponent.

This completes the training section using the jab as your counter weapon. Obviously, there are hundreds of other variations of these drills but these represent a good starting point. As a beginner, you should train these drills until you feel that you are at a level at which they work effectively for you. Once you are at that stage, move on to the next set of training drills.

The more experienced fighter might want to move straight on to the next section although it is always good practice to re-cap the basics to ensure your foundations are strong.

Counter a Punch Using a Cross

The principles of the following drills are the same as those that apply when countering with a jab. The only difference is that this time you are using the cross punch instead of the jab as your attacking tool.

Drill 1 – Cover and Counter

As before, your partner throws a straight punch (in this case a jab), which you defend using a double arm block or cover (Fig 281). As he retracts his punch, follow straight back with a cross punch (Fig 282). As before, you need to start thinking of this as a movement with one beat (cover and punch) as opposed to two beats (cover pause and punch). If you pause for a second you give your opponent enough time to return with another attack.

Drill 2 – Slip and Counter to Body

As your partner throws his jab, slip to the left to evade the attack (Fig 283) and, at the same time,

Fig 281 Cover the attack.

Fig 282 Counter with a cross.

Fig 283 Slip the jab.

Fig 284 Cross to the body.

drop and cross punch to the area he has just exposed (Fig 284). With a little speed, you should still be able to hit the target before he has time to retract his arm fully.

Drill 3 – Slip and Counter to Body, Version 2
The same defence and counter works if your opponent decides to throw a cross punch rather than a jab (Figs 285 and 286).

Fig 285 Slip the cross.

Fig 286 Cross to the body.

Fig 287 Parry the cross.

Fig 288 Cross to the head.

Fig 289 Parry the cross.

Fig 290 Cross to the body.

Drill 4 – Parry and Counter to Head

This time your partner throws a cross punch to your head. Parry the attack with a slight shift left (without actually moving your feet; it is just a body shift) (Fig 287). At the same time, cross punch over the top of the arm (Fig 288). The technique has been slightly over-exaggerated to help you understand the movement here; in reality, your opponent would actually be retracting his arm back from the cross as your punch lands, which should, theoretically, make it easier for you.

Drill 5 – Parry and Counter to the Body

As with the previous drill, you can also opt to counter-punch to the body. The movements are exactly the same but, instead of reaching over your opponent's attacking arm to counter to the head, you simply drop slightly to bring you in line with the body and attack here instead (Figs 289 to 290).

Drill 6 – Evasion and Counter

This time your opponent throws a rear hooking punch to your head. As you see the punch come in, drop and roll underneath (*see* page 76), so the punch sails over your head (Fig 291). This action will put you in line with your opponent's body so, as you roll out of the evasion, send your cross punch directly towards their mid line (Fig 292). The movement of the evasion here will help to give additional power to the punch if done correctly.

Drill 7 – Lean-Back Counter

Your opponent throws a rear hooking punch attack to the head. As you see the punch come in, lean back out of the way, transferring your body weight on to your rear foot and keeping the chin tucked firmly behind the lead shoulder with the rear hand slightly forward to protect the opposite

Fig 291 Roll and evade a hook.

Fig 292 Cross to the body.

Fig 293 Lean back to evade a hook.

Fig 294 Cross from the angle.

side (Fig 293). At the same time as leaning back to evade the hook, send a cross punch straight out to your opponent's chin (Fig 294).

The angle of the body with this counter-strike is far from the traditional position associated with the cross. This is what separates a good fighter from an average fighter. In the fight game, you sometimes need to be able to break away from the traditional method of throwing a technique and instead adapt the technique to make it work from any angle or range. This is covered later in the book, but now is a good point at which to begin to understand an important principle.

Drill 8 – Block and Counter

This drill is one for all the point fighters and is a very popular defence and counter with fighters of this style. It can also be adopted for use by the continuous fighter but there is an inherent risk that moving the arm so far away from the head or body could reduce the overall defence capabilities for this type of fighter.

As your opponent throws a jab or backfist strike to your head, intercept his attack by bringing your lead forearm up, knocking his punch off target (Fig 295). At the same time, drop slightly and perform a reverse punch or cross punch to the gap you have just exposed (Fig 296). As with the other drills, try not to think of this as a two-beat move, as this will slow it down. Instead, you block and counter at the same time so, as soon as your opponent commits to his attack, the next thing he knows is that you have hit him.

Counter a Punch Using a Hook

Drill 1 – Evasion and Counter to the Body

In a left-lead fighting stance, your opponent swings a lead hooking punch towards your head. As you see the punch come in, roll underneath it, using your footwork and body mechanics correctly (Fig 297). As you roll out of the evasion, send a lead hooking punch to the body of your opponent, using the twisting motion you created with your evasion to generate speed and power (Fig 298).

Fig 295 Rising block defence against a straight punch.

Fig 296 Cross to the body.

Fig 297 Evade a lead hook.

Fig 298 Hook to the body.

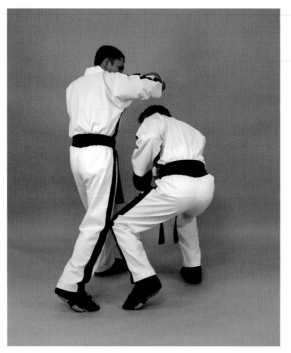

Fig 299 Evade a rear hook.

Fig 300 Counter with a hook to the body.

Fig 301 Lean back to evade the jab.

Fig 302 Hook to the head.

Drill 2 – Evasion and Counter to the Body, Version 2

This time your opponent throws a rear hooking punch to the head. Drop and roll in the opposite direction to the last drill in order to evade the hook (Fig 299). As you roll out of the evasion you now attack with a rear hooking punch to the body (Fig 300).

Drill 3 – Lean-Back Evasion

As your opponent performs a jab to the head, lean back to evade the attack, keeping your chin tucked tightly behind your lead shoulder and your rear hand in position (Fig 301). At the same time, zone out slightly with your lead leg in order to bring you in closer to your opponent and change your angle; as you do, hook to your opponent's head with your lead arm (Fig 302). Try to make the lean, zone and hook as fast as possible; if you can perform this as one motion, there is a greater likelihood that the counter will land.

Drill 4 – Slip and Counter

This time your opponent throws a cross punch to your head. As the punch comes in, slip to the left to evade the attack (Fig 303). Transfer your body weight on to your lead leg and lean in deep, hooking to the body with your lead arm at the same time (Fig 304). The rear hand comes back up to cover the chin (*see* Fig 304), just in case your opponent decides to follow with a hooking punch of his own. Theoretically, though, yours should land first.

Drill 5 – Zone Right and Counter

Do not confuse the zone and the slip as being the same technique. Although they look very similar, they are actually very different movements. This time your opponent throws a jab to the head. As the punch comes in, step out at a 45-degree angle (zone out) with your rear leg (Fig 305). As you do this, aim a well-placed rear hook towards the body of your opponent (Fig 306). If he exposes the back, and the rules allow, then you are in a perfect position to target the kidney area. Just be aware that not all competitions allow this area to be included as a scoring zone.

Note how much closer you are to your opponent using this zone-out method (Fig 305), compared

Fig 303 Slip the cross.

Fig 304 Hook to the body.

with simply slipping his attack (Fig 303) in the previous drill.

Drill 6 – Zone Left and Counter

For this drill to work, your opponent throws a cross punch to your head. This time you zone left

Fig 305 Zone right to evade the jab.

Fig 306 Hook to the body.

Fig 307 Zone left to evade the cross punch.

Fig 308 Hook to the body.

to avoid the attack (Fig 307) and deliver a hooking punch to the body using your lead hand (Fig 308). This variation on the zone gives you a greater understanding of how you can use the same simple step to move left or right, depending on which attack is thrown at you. Do not get confused by this though. It is still possible to zone right to avoid a cross punch in the same way as you can zone left and avoid a jab. The variation in punches between the two drills just gives you another way of working the defence.

Counter a Punch Using an Uppercut

The uppercut as a counter-attack is a technique that is often under-used, particularly by the less experienced fighter, who is thus missing out on another incredible weapon. The striking angle of the uppercut means that it can enter areas that no other punch can and from all sorts of incredible angles, so leaving it out through a lack of understanding could have dire consequences in a fight.

Drill 1 – Slip Right and Counter

As your opponent throws his jab, slip to the right, covering the chin with your lead hand, and chamber the rear hand in preparation for the uppercut (Fig 309). With the jab extended, use your new angle of attack to uppercut underneath his arm, aiming for the chin with your rear hand (Fig 310).

The beauty with this type of attack is that you temporarily step outside of the danger zone and use the opponent's striking arm as a psychological barrier between you and him. It is true that from this position he could probably throw a rear hooking punch from this angle, but you could also roll underneath that and counter once more.

Drill 2 – Slip Left and Counter

This time your opponent throws a cross punch. As you see the punch come in, slip left to evade the attack. As you move, keep your rear hand on your chin and chamber your lead hand in readiness for the counter (Fig 311). As before, drive your lead hand up, underneath their arm striking the chin with the lead uppercut (Fig 312).

Fig 309 Slip to the right to avoid the jab.

Fig 310 Uppercut underneath the arm.

Fig 311 Slip left to avoid the attack.

Fig 312 Uppercut to the chin.

Fig 313 Slip right and counter to the body.

Fig 314 Slip left and uppercut to the body.

Drill 3 – Slip Right and Counter to the Body

Take the principles from the previous two drills and, instead of punching to the head, attack to the body (Fig 313).

Drill 4 – Slip Left and Counter to the Body

As your opponent throws his cross punch, slip to the left and uppercut to the body with your lead hand (Fig 314).

Drill 5 – Single Cover and Counter

This time your opponent throws a rear hooking punch to your head. Bring your lead hand up to cover the attack and at the same time send your rear uppercut out towards his chin (Fig 315).

Drill 6 – Single Cover and Counter, Version 2

This time your opponent throws a lead hooking punch towards your head. Bring your rear arm up to cover the attack so the punch bounces off and

at the same time drive your lead uppercut out towards his chin (Fig 316). This particular counter is also very effective when used with movement. Pivoting on the lead foot, and swinging the rear foot round in a clockwise motion, will change your angle and force your opponent to turn to face you, buying you a second or two to add a few more counters.

Drill 7 – Lean-Back and Counter

From your fighting stance your opponent throws a jab towards your head. Lean back, moving your head out of the way of the attack, but keeping your feet in position (otherwise you will be too far away to counter), and keep your chin covered with your lead hand. At the same time, drive a rear uppercut out towards his body (Fig 317).

Drill 8 – Lean-Back and Counter, Version 2

The final drill shows how to use the same lean-back defence, countering with a lead uppercut to the body. In the figure, the initial attack from your

Fig 315 Single-arm cover and uppercut counter.

Fig 316 Cover a lead attack and uppercut counter to the head.

Fig 317 Lean back to evade the jab and rear uppercut to the body.

Fig 318 Lean back to evade the jab and lead uppercut to the body.

opponent is still the jab, however, any straight-punch attack would be fine in order to practise this evasion and counter drill (Fig 318).

Work your way through all the training drills in this section taking each one in turn and training it until you feel confident enough to use it in sparring. Be careful not to rush through the drills simply to get to the end. Instead, take your time, methodically working through each one, tweaking it if you feel you need to so that it works for you.

Remember, you need to train something over a thousand times before you really begin to understand how it works.

10 Counters Against Kicks Using Punches

When you are venturing out on your sparring journey for the first time it can feel as though you are starting all over again. I have been a kickboxing and martial art instructor for many years now, and students have told me time and time again that, regardless of how much experience they have working out in the gym or dojo, when they first enter the world of sparring they all feel that they move back in to the role of beginner. Although it has been a while since I first started sparring, I can fully understand their feelings and concerns and I am able to re-live my own experiences through theirs. It does not matter how much experience you have punching pads or working out on a punch bag, the second you put those boxing gloves on for the first time, you start off again as a white belt.

For that reason, using a punch to beat a kick can seem like a daunting task, particularly if you *are* new to sparring. In theory, the kicker has a slight advantage over the puncher when it comes to sparring because of distance. As the legs are generally longer than the arms, the kicker need only stay out of the reach of the opponent's arms to prevent the attacking punches from connecting and yet he also needs to be close enough in order to land his own kicks (*see* page 79, Chapter 8, Defence against Kicks, for a better understanding of distance). Despite this unwritten rule, it is still possible for the punch to beat the kick; you just need to understand how to do it.

The following drills will take each of the static kicks in turn and look at ways of using the punch to out-perform the kick. The drills involve you receiving an attack first, defending that attack and then returning it with a counter-attack of your own. However, you need to be aware that in a real fight, be it competitive or in the street, the fight rarely takes on this neat form. More likely than not, you will receive multiple attacks from your opponent, mixed up with kicks and punches, which will make your job of defending and countering much more difficult. For the purposes of training, you will focus on a single attack, defence and counter to begin with. Then, as you become increasingly confident with this drill, you can introduce more realism in the form of two, three or four attacks, when you feel ready.

Counter Against the Front Kick

When defending against a kick, it is important to understand that you need to use distance and timing to land your counter-attack. In some cases the distance and/or the timing might not be quite right, and countering with a punch will not be the most effective option. The following drills use the perfect conditions but in reality you will need to evaluate each situation as it unfolds in order to determine the best course of action. You will need to consider a number of issues:

- How close are you to your opponent?
- What are they attacking with?
- Which foot is bearing most of your weight?
- Which way are you travelling?
- What is your current body position?

As a result of asking yourself these questions, you will then need to determine which is the best form of defence (cover, parry, evade, side-step, move), as well as the selecting the best form of counter-attack – should you kick and if so which kick would work best, or should you punch and if so do you jab, cross or hook? And all this needs to be done in a millisecond. It does all come in time, but it will not happen overnight and not without a great deal of practice on your part.

Fig 319 Defend the front-kick attack.

Fig 320 Counter with a jab.

Fig 321 Parry the front-kick attack.

Fig 322 Counter with a jab.

Drill 1 – Cover and Counter

Your opponent attacks using a mid-line front kick. Defend the kick using a double-forearm cover (Fig 319). Keep the gloves tight against the face and the elbows in close to the body to help absorb the attack, but at the same time ensure you can see over the top of your gloves. As your opponent withdraws the kick, explode in using your jab to attack the head and utilizing a simple step forwards to cover the distance (Fig 320).

Drill 2 – Parry and Counter

As your opponent attacks with the front kick, use your rear hand to parry the attack, knocking the kick off the attacking line and at the same time turning your opponent away from you (Fig 321). You could have parried this one using your lead hand but that would have opened you up for a second attack (a cross punch, for example) from your opponent. This way you buy yourself a second to counter-attack as your opponent now needs to adjust his body position in order to bring himself

back into the fight. From here, send out a jab to the head as your opponent recovers (Fig 322).

Drill 3 – Shin Block and Counter

This defence is very effective, but it is advisable to train it until you can competently pull it off before using it for real. The danger is that, if your balance is not good and your energy is not right, the attack from your opponent may well knock you off balance. You may not necessarily fall over, but you will need to regain your composure and this could give your opponent a few free shots that you may not be able to defend against. It could even end up costing you the fight.

As the front kick comes in, bring your lead leg up to defend the attack using your shin. Lean into the attack to help absorb it; this should also reduce the possibility of you getting knocked back while up on one leg (Fig 323). Now, as you go to land the leg back down, zone out slightly and counter with a cross punch as your leg touches down (Fig 324).

Fig 323 Shin block the front-kick attack.

Fig 324 Counter with a cross.

Drill 4 – Step In and Counter

This technique involves absorbing the attack by stepping into it at exactly the right moment. Your timing is helped by your opponent's inability to disguise his attack and consequently telegraphing his movements. Key tell-tale signs that a kick is coming might include a slight step with the back foot (generally done to cover distance or because the weight distribution is incorrect), or an adjustment of hip position on the kicking side. There are a thousand other possible giveaways that you need to look for and learn as the fight progresses, to help you develop your ability to counter a kicking attack from your opponent. As soon as you see a sign that he is about to kick, step into the attack and counter-punch at the same time (Fig 325).

With this type of counter it is important to understand that you step and attack together. If you step, pause and attack, you add an extra beat to the drill and there is a chance that your opponent will take advantage of that pause and get a second attack in. You also need to make sure you absorb the attack with the correct part of your body (in this case your forearm). As you can imagine, if you get this wrong the consequences could be quite painful.

Counter from a Round Kick

The round kick is an incredibly versatile kick, which works equally as well low section as it does high section, but there are a number of ways of defending and countering against it. The following drills focus predominantly on defending against a high-section attack.

Drill 1 – Cover and Counter

As your opponent attacks to the head using his lead leg, bring your rear hand (which should be on the chin already) up higher to defend. The motion of bringing the hand up higher is done to protect the temple, which is one of the knockout zones on the body. It does not matter too much if the blow glances off the top of the head but you do need to

Fig 325 Step in and jab together.

Fig 326 Cover the round-kick attack.

Fig 327 Counter with a cross.

Fig 328 Step in and cross together.

ensure you protect the temple and the chin (which will now be covered by the forearm) from an attack (Fig 326). As your opponent retracts the leg, zone out slightly with your lead leg and counter with a cross punch to the chin (Fig 327).

Drill 2 – Step In and Counter

This next drill is very effective due to the speed of the counter. As your opponent attacks to the head with his lead leg, cover the kick with your rear hand as before but this time step in at the same time and counter using a jab (Fig 328). As before, with this counter you need to make sure you move in to absorb the attack at the same time as landing your counter-punch. Once your opponent has committed to his kick it is very difficult (although not impossible) for him to punch; even if he is sufficiently skilled to punch at the same time as kicking with one foot off the ground, there is little likelihood that there will be enough energy behind the punch to deliver any serious power.

Drill 3 – Shin Block and Counter

The shin block can be used as a defence against a front kick, but it is probably at its most effective against a round kick. The round kick can be amazingly damaging, because it travels in a circular motion, but it is unlikely to knock you over in the same way as a straight kick (front kick or side kick, for example) can, unless of course it catches you on a knockout zone, but this is a completely different thing. For this reason it is highly recommended that you use a shin block as a defence against a low-level round kick; if your flexibility and timing allows, it can also work well against a mid-line attack.

As your opponent attacks with the lead leg, bring your rear leg up so you stop the kick from landing using your shin (Fig 329). Keep your guard tight and remember to form a rear shield using your forearm and fist at the same time. As your opponent retracts the kick, follow through with a cross punch to the chin (Fig 330).

Fig 329 Shin block the round kick.

Fig 330 Cross punch to counter.

Fig 331 Lean back to evade the kick.

Fig 332 Rear uppercut to counter.

Drill 4 – Lean-Back and Counter

If you have trained the drills so far, you will know that it is better not to get hit at all than to take the hits even on the arms or the shins. Therefore, this defence is a good one and works well against a round kick. As your opponent attacks, transfer your body weight on to your rear leg and lean backwards out of the way of the attack (Fig 331). As your opponent starts to retract his leg in order to land it, move back in, in order to follow his leg down and this time use a rear uppercut to attack the chin (Fig 322). You could also use a cross punch for this particular counter-attack but it is a good idea to vary your drills, so try working with an uppercut instead this time.

Drill 5 – Evade and Counter

Providing you are quick enough, the roll-and-recover-style evasion, which was used earlier to counter a punch attack, should be a very effective defence against a round kick. The motion of the kick is very similar to that of the hooking punch, which may be defended in the same way.

Fig 334 Roll underneath the leg.

Fig 333 Duck and roll to avoid the kick.

Fig 335 Uppercut to counter as you reset yourself.

As the kick comes in, drop to avoid it hitting the head (Fig 333). As it passes above you, roll underneath your opponent's leg so you end up on the opposite side of it. This in turn will make it difficult for your opponent to land a second attack (Fig 334). As he lands the leg and looks to recover, send a rear uppercut up towards the chin (Fig 335). The uppercut is probably the most effective counterpunch from this slightly crouched position as you can explode up with it quite smoothly.

Remember: when countering an attack, you should try to use the most effective counter based on your body position. As you are travelling in a certain way with the roll-and-recover-style evasion, flow with it. When the body travels in a circular anti-clockwise motion, as with this evasion, the most natural flowing technique to follow with would probably be a rear hooking punch. You could certainly generate a great deal of speed and power using the circular motion of the evasion.

However, there is a chance with this defence that the opponent's head, which is ultimately what you are targeting with your counter-attack, could be too far away for a rear hooking punch to land. In this case, an uppercut would probably be the next most effective technique. It also works well from this position, with the added advantage that it can also be used very effectively from mid or even long range. This line of travel does not flow as well with the hooking punch as it is essentially more of a close-range technique.

Drill 6 – Absorb and Counter
This drill involves absorbing the attack by spinning into it, using the forearms to block with at the same time. As your partner kicks, turn into the attack using your forearms to cover the head as if using a double-forearm-style block, and step across the centre line with your lead leg (Fig 336). This should, hopefully, be enough to stop the attack and take away any power it may have had. At the same time, continue to turn in order to set up your counter and, as you spin out of the defence, use a spinning backfist to attack the head of your opponent as he retracts his leg (Fig 337).

To assist with the spinning backfist, you might want to bring your rear leg (in this case your right leg) round, so you can generate more power in the

Fig 336 Absorb the round kick.

Fig 337 Spinning back fist strike to counter.

Fig 338 Zone left to evade the attack.

Fig 339 Lead uppercut to counter.

Fig 340 Use the universal block to defend against the attack.

Fig 341 Back fist as the kick is retracted.

strike. At the same time, ensure you are not off balance by maintaining a good wide base.

Drill 7 – Zone and Counter

A simple zone and counter-attack will take you off the centre line and bring you in close for a lead uppercut. As your partner kicks, step out at a 45-degree angle with your lead leg (Fig 338). Keep your head covered with your rear hand just in case the kick follows through. From here, you should be close enough to use your lead uppercut before your opponent has the chance to land his leg and get a second attack in (Fig 339).

Counters Against the Side Kick

The side kick is designed to attack in a straight line with the kicker standing in a side-on position. Most of the time, the kick will attack front on – meaning the front of the body – but this could seem not to be the case if your opponent is standing sideways, as it would then appear to be attacking the side of the body. Do not take the term 'side kick' as literal; it is used simply to help you understand the line of travel for the kick. It is also probably most effective when used to attack the mid line as opposed to the low or high line, as there is generally more energy behind a kick that travels parallel to the floor.

Drill 1 – Block and Counter

Utilizing the universal block from earlier, bring your lead arm across your body and your rear hand up tight, slightly in front of the chin. It is also a good idea to tuck the other side of your chin behind your lead shoulder to protect all the main target areas from attack (Fig 340). As the kick bounces off your lead arm, explode forwards and counter with a backfist strike or possibly a jab (depending on your opponent's guard) (Fig 341).

Drill 2 – Block and Counter, Version 2

This second version works well when you are in more of a front-on position and your opponent attacks with a mid-line side kick. As the kick comes in, bring your arms together in order to block the attack (Fig 342). From here your lead arm is in the perfect position to send out a jab as your opponent retracts the kick (Fig 343).

Fig 342 Double forearm block to defend against the kick.

Fig 343 Jab to the head as the leg is retracted.

As you jab, step into the punch. This will not only add more power to the technique, but will also mean that, if your opponent decides to send out a second side kick without landing his leg to the area you have now exposed, this will bring your body in too close for the kick to have any real effect. The principle is the same as when you stepped in close to absorb a kick earlier. (For more on multiple kicks, *see* page 181.)

Drill 3 – Evasion and Counter

For this drill to work you will need to have fast footwork, both to evade the attack and land the counter. From your fighting stance (Fig 344), as your partner chambers his leg in readiness for the kick, step back with your lead leg (Fig 345). As he extends his leg to execute the kick, step back with your rear leg (Fig 346). If you have done it properly, you should now be out of range of his kick, but keep a universal block in place, just in case. As

he retracts his leg, push off your rear leg and explode in with a cross punch to the chin (Fig 347).

Drill 4 – Step-In and Counter

The step-in counters are very effective methods of defending against a kick, particularly if the opponent is quite adept at giving away what he is going to do. Care is needed with this one, however; if you rush into this defence, you stand a good chance of receiving a knee to the rib cage (*see* Fig 349 for an exaggerated example of this). The best part of the opponent's leg to connect with for this defence is the shin, using your lead leg to absorb the attack. Therefore you need to have lightning reflexes, to step in and close the distance, preventing him from chambering the leg in order to kick. At the same time as stepping in, jab to the chin to counter the attack. Figs 348 and 349 show this defence in motion.

Fig 344 Face your opponent.

Fig 345 Step back with your lead leg.

Fig 346 Step back with your rear leg.

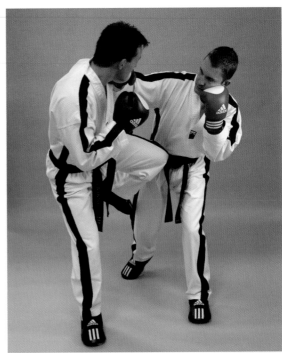

Fig 347 Explode with a cross punch to counter.

Fig 348 Face your opponent.

Fig 349 Step in to absorb the attack and counter at the same time.

Fig 350 Step back to evade the attack.

Fig 351 Explode in to counter as the leg is retracted.

Fig 352 Parry the hook kick with your rear hand.

Fig 353 Jab to the head to counter the attack.

Drill 5 – Evasion and Counter

As your opponent kicks, transfer your body weight on to your back foot and, by bending your rear leg, lean out of the way of the attack, keeping a universal block in place just in case of a multiple side-kick attack (Fig 350). As your opponent retracts the kick, spring off your rear leg, striking with a backfist or jab to the head (Fig 351).

Counters Against the Hooking Kick

It can be awkward to defend against the hooking kick; because of its angle, it is not an attack that you often expect. For that reason, it is certainly worth developing, similarly, it is also worth gaining an understanding of it, and learning how to defend against it.

Drill 1 – Parry and Counter

As your opponent performs a lead-leg hooking kick to the head, parry the kick by bringing your rear hand across your body in order to meet the kick with the palm of your rear hand (Fig 352). You could also use the closed fist of a boxing glove to parry with if you prefer. As you parry the leg, push it over the top of your lead shoulder so that you create an opening for the jab to find its mark (Fig 353).

Drill 2 – Evasion and Counter

As your opponent executes the lead hooking kick, drop slightly and roll underneath the leg (Fig 354). As he continues through with his kick, continue to roll, using your feet to turn you so that you appear on the inside of his body (Fig 355). From here, fire out a cross punch to his body, keeping your head away from his weapons and your guard tight to your chin (Fig 356).

Drill 3 – Step In and Counter

The step-in defence for the hooking kick is a little different from the step-in defences previously covered, simply because the opponent's leg can act as a natural barrier between you and him. For this reason, the counter-punches available to you for returning the attack are slightly limited, although the ones that do comfortably fit the gap are very

Fig 354 Drop to evade the kick.

Fig 355 Roll under the leg.

Fig 356 Cross punch to the body to counter.

effective. As your opponent attempts to kick, keep your guard tight and step into the kick so that his attack is absorbed by your back and the striking part of his foot passes behind you.

At the same time, by keeping your guard high you should now be able to jab over the top of his leg and comfortably find the chin (Fig 357). Just be sure to keep your rear guard up, as there is the possibility of receiving a lead hooking punch off your opponent from this close-range position.

Drill 4 – Lean-Back and Counter
As your opponent kicks, transfer your weight on to your rear leg and lean back out of the way of the kick (Fig 358). As the kick passes over or in front of you, spring off your rear leg and either backfist or jab to your opponent's head (Fig 359).

Drill 5 – Cover and Counter
The final drill to complete the hooking kick defence and counters involves using a lead-hand single-arm cover to defend against the kick. Try grabbing the back of your neck with this defence, to ensure that you are properly covered. Although

Fig 357 Step in to absorb the attack and jab at the same time.

Fig 358 Lead back to evade the kick.

Fig 359 Explode in with a backfist to the head.

Fig 360 Defend against the kick with a single-arm cover.

there is little risk of the hooking kick penetrating the smaller gaps in your defences, any time you use this block it is worth ensuring you do it properly (Fig 360).

As the kick bounces off the guard, keep your left hand in place – you can even use this to control where the kick lands by pushing the kick down as you turn into the punch – and cross punch to the head (Fig 361).

Fig 361 Cross punch as the kick is retracted.

Counters Against the Axe Kick

The axe kick is one of the most effective kicks in the kickboxing syllabus. Although it might not generate the knockout power of some of the other kicks, if done properly it is actually very difficult to defend. The following drills might change that for you, should you ever get attacked in this way.

Drill 1 – Block and Counter
As your opponent kicks, time it right and perform a lead-arm rising block to prevent the kick from

landing (Fig 362). From here, you can either drive the leg back down towards the floor by sliding the kick off your blocking arm; alternatively, you can drive forwards, keeping the kick on your arm, and force your opponent off balance, causing them to fall over and generating a takedown.

A fighter's use of this technique should depend of course on the rules to which he is fighting. On occasion, however, even if the rules do not allow takedowns, certain fighters will use this kind of tactic regardless – at least until they are told to stop. It can demoralize an opponent, which in turn can cause him psychologically to lose the fight. It will also wear an opponent down, as it can be quite tiring repeatedly picking yourself up off the floor.

For this drill, however, you will simply slide the leg off the arm and cross punch to the chin to complete the drill (Fig 363).

Drill 2 – Step-In and Counter

This defence works well with the axe kick, as the kick relies on the opponent staying in the kicking range. It is also very difficult to recover from this defence as you are very vulnerable to over-balancing (as in the previous drill). As you step in close to absorb this kick, the calf or thigh of the leg, depending on how deep you step in and how flexible your opponent is, will make contact with your lead shoulder and the striking part (the heel) will pass harmlessly behind the head (Fig 364).

From here, simply drive the leg to the floor by twisting with your lead shoulder and, at the same time, cross punch to the head to finish (Fig 365).

Drill 3 – Block and Counter

This time as the kick comes in bring your lead hand up to cover the head using the single-arm block as before. If done properly, the axe kick will

Fig 362 Rising block to defend against the kick.

Fig 363 Cross punch to counter.

Fig 364 Step in to counter the kick.

Fig 365 Cross punch to counter.

Fig 366 Single-arm defence against the axe kick.

Fig 367 Cross punch to the body to counter.

connect with the arm instead of the head (Fig 366). Drive the leg off by twisting out (drop your lead shoulder towards the floor) and finish with a cross punch to the body (Fig 367). You could also opt to attack the head with this counter depending on where your opponent's guard is after you clear the kick.

Drill 4 – Parry and Counter

This final drill for the axe-kick defence and counter is not for the faint-hearted. It relies on your ability to judge distance and timing, which, if you have only just entered the world of sparring, might need a bit more work. For that reason it is certainly worth training this drill so that you begin to understand it better. However, it is not recommended that you try it in a competitive environment until you can competently, as well as confidently, pull it off in training.

As the kick comes in, use your lead shoulder to parry it and drive it to the ground (Fig 368). This takes good timing and confidence so ensure your partner slows the kick right down as you train it. As your opponent attempts to regain his balance, continue spinning in a clockwise (depending on which leg you have in front, of course) direction, and strike using a spinning backfist to the head (Fig 369).

Counters Against the Outside Crescent Kick

In the right circumstances, this kick can be a very effective weapon, but it is rarely used in competitive fighting because it draws you in a little too close to your opponent. A little-known fact about this kick is that it is actually designed for close range, in areas where you would probably be more likely to use a punch than a kick. For that reason, and because it demands a considerable amount of flexibility, it is often used only by the most experienced kickers.

Drill 1 – Block and Counter

As your opponent steps up to kick, bring your lead arm up as if you were grabbing the back of your neck (Fig 370). As he retracts his kick, or as it bounces off your defence, keep your guard in

Fig 368 Use the shoulder to parry the kick.

Fig 369 Spinning backfist to counter the attack.

place and strike using a cross punch to the body or head (Fig 371).

Keep in mind that this kick travels across the body in a similar way to the axe kick. However, unlike the axe kick, which travels from the ceiling to the floor and is more likely to land on the top of the head, the outside crescent kick travels from wall to wall and is designed to strike the side of the head.

Fig 370 Use a single-arm cover to defend against the kick.

Fig 371 Cross punch to the body as the kick is retracted.

Fig 372 Parry the kick using the rear hand.

Fig 373 Jab to the head as the leg is retracted.

Drill 2 – Parry and Counter

As your opponent attacks, bring your rear hand out in front to parry the kick and prevent it from landing. Just be sure to keep your head tucked safely behind your blocking arm (Fig 372). From here, push the kick away to clear it and bring your lead hand over the top of the leg as it lands, and jab to the head (Fig 373).

Drill 3 – Step-In and Counter

As with all the step-in defences, timing is key. As soon as you see your opponent start to kick, step in close so that the attack gets absorbed by your body and the leg does not have enough time to build up any energy or find its mark. The leg bounces harmlessly off your lead shoulder (*see* Fig 374), while the striking part passes way too far behind to do any damage. In addition, if your opponent makes the mistake of dropping his guard as he kicks, you can counter with a very effective cross punch to the head (Fig 375).

Drill 4 – Lean-Back and Counter

An evasion and counter is a type of defence that works well against an outside crescent kick and means of course that you do not need to receive the hit in any way, which is always better. As your opponent executes the kick, simply lean back out of the way so the leg passes right in front of you. You can do this quite successfully without the need to shuffle-step back or move the feet in any way (Fig 376). As the leg crosses the centre line, explode in with a jab to the head (Fig 377).

The timing is important here once again, as you ideally want to catch your opponent while he is recovering from the kick. If you pause, he will have a chance to land the leg, which in turn means that he will be able to regain his composure and possibly evade your attack.

Counters Against the Inside Crescent Kick

An attack from an inside crescent kick works along a similar plane of trajectory to that of the outside crescent kick; the only difference is that it travels in the opposite direction. Of the two kicks, the outside version is probably the more defensive

Fig 374 Step in to absorb the kick.

Fig 375 Cross punch to counter the attack.

135

Fig 376 Lean back to evade the attack.

Fig 377 Jab to the head as the kick is retracted.

as the motion of crossing your own body with the leg acts as a defence in itself. On the other hand, the direction of travel with the inside crescent kick has a tendency to open the body, making it more of a target to the opponent.

Drill 1 – Block and Counter

As your opponent kicks, bring your rear arm up to defend the head, grabbing the back of the neck as you do (Fig 378). It is likely that the opponent will attack with the lead leg more so than the rear leg, although, if he does switch his attacking side, you can simply block with your other arm. As you defend the kick, the leg will either bounce off your guard or the opponent will retract it. As soon as this happens, send a jab straight out to his head (Fig 379). Be sure to explode with the counter so that your opponent does not have the time to land his leg and regain his composure.

Drill 2 – Parry and Counter

As the attack comes in, bring your lead hand up to meet the kick and knock it off its attacking line. Be sure to keep your head off the centre line (you move it as you parry), and tuck it behind the defending hand as you block (Fig 380). From here, push the leg out of the way, forcing your opponent to land it, and cross punch over the top of the leg to either the body or the head (Fig 381).

Drill 3 – Block and Counter

For this block, you use the inner forearm and set up a spinning counter-attack. As your opponent kicks, hit the leg with the inner forearm of the lead hand in the same way as you would if you were going to parry it (Fig 382). In order to pull the next move off you need to ensure you spin into the defence as you block the kick, to give you the momentum for the counter. As your opponent retracts the leg, continue to spin, aiming to strike with a spinning backfist to the head while your opponent attempts to recover (Fig 383).

The reason you block with the forearm for this defence and not the palm as in the case of the parry, is due to the counter. The forearm has a much larger surface area and, as you then spin out of the defence without pausing, there is a risk in using the palm that you could misjudge the kick

Fig 378 Use a single-arm cover to block the attack.

Fig 379 Jab to the head as the kick is retracted.

Fig 380 Parry the kick with the lead hand.

Fig 381 Cross punch to the head to counter.

and miss blocking it completely. Of course, this could have disastrous consequences.

Counters Against the Spinning Kick

It would be very easy to get lost in this drill and simply put a spin on every kick covered. However, by now you should really have grasped the various ways in which to defend and counter a basic kick.

The principle is always the same, and the real skill lies in deciding, in an instant, which is the most appropriate method of defending the attack. The decision is based on all the contributing factors and for that reason this process cannot be choreographed. Instead, you simply need to train yourself to react instantaneously, through repetition of all the drills, so that when the attack comes you can defend it, regardless of your position, weight distribution, stance and body angle.

The following drills deal with two simple spinning kick attacks and two simple methods of countering them.

Drill 1 – Block and Counter a Spinning Hook Kick

The spinning hook kick is an incredibly powerful kick and, employed by a skilled kicker who understands timing, it can be very dangerous. If it is done properly, the spinning hook kick will cause you some trauma should you receive it on your guard, so you need to be aware of a simple way of defending the kick, which in turn will set up your opponent for a great counter-strike.

Keeping yourself tightly covered (chin tucked firmly behind your lead shoulder, rear hand covering the opposite side), as the kick comes round, simply lean back out of the way (Fig 384). The process of leaning back should cause your opponent to continue through with the kick or, at the very least, pass it over your head with a view to landing it again. At this exact point, you fire out a cross punch to the body or head – this is the moment at which your opponent is likely to be at his most vulnerable (Fig 385). As you counter, be sure to keep your guard tight; there is a small chance that a skilled kicker will deliver a round

Fig 382 Spin into the attack using the forearm to block.

Fig 383 Spinning backfist to counter the attack.

Fig 384 Lean out of the way of the spinning kick.

kick (right leg) as a counter-measure against such a counter-attack.

Drill 2 – Block and Counter a Spinning Back Kick

This drill works along a similar line to the previous one where you use the opponent's attempt to recover from the kick as your opportunity to counter it. As the spinning back kick comes in, use a universal block to stop it from hitting your body (Fig 386). Then, as the opponent retracts his leg and attempts to recover from the attack, explode in with a cross punch to the head or body (Fig 387).

Although the spinning back kick is incredibly powerful, it involves the attacker turning his back at the exact time that his kick lands. As a result, if he fails to score with the kick, or to knock you backwards with it should you manage to block it, it can be relatively easy to counter, particularly as all his other weapons should now be facing away from you at the point of impact.

Fig 385 Cross punch to the body as the kick travels past.

Fig 386 Use a universal block to defend the spinning back kick.

Fig 387 Cross punch as the kicking leg lands.

The Psychology of Training

Take each training section, starting with the front kick and working through to the spinning kicks, and work it in isolation, covering each training drill one at a time. Variations in defences for each kick are given, to ensure that you understand how to adapt your block in case you find yourself in an unfamiliar position.

If you train to block an attack only one way and then find yourself in a position that does not allow you to use that block, you will inevitably come unstuck. Understanding several different defences, and training to use a number of counters against the same attack, will increase your chances of defending yourself in all situations.

The important factor is, of course, the speed at which you can process all the information your brain is taking in at that exact second in the fight.

Based on the main principles – your body position, weight distribution, hand position, and so on – you then have to react as quickly as possible to use the defence that is the most appropriate, based on how you are standing, as well as the most suitable counter-attack based on the target available. You should be able not only to identify your target – your opponent's head or body – but also the exact place on the head or body that you can attack, based on the way in which your opponent is holding his guard.

This is the difference between the white belt (beginner) and the black belt (advanced) student. The processing speed of the advanced student is greater than that of the beginner, because years of repetitive training develop skills and abilities to such a level that many of the intricate details of a movement or process can be done automatically, without the need for conscious thought.

It is not unlike riding a bike or driving a car. When you first start out to learn this new skill you have to make a conscious effort to think about everything you do, just to get moving. The bike is a great example, as it is not dissimilar to kickboxing, in that it requires an understanding of body position, balance and the way in which your hands and feet work together to prevent you getting hurt (in this case, falling off). After a few months, you can get the bike moving, stay on and even enjoy the ride without having to think too much about it; getting going is by now automatic.

Thereafter, further success and your ultimate achievement depend on the amount of time spent riding that bike. Although you might never aspire to win the Tour de France, this example should help you relate to something that you will have previously experienced. Hopefully you still remember what it was like to learn to ride a bike, and to develop this new skill. Through a combination of muscle memory and locking it in to the body's nervous system via repetition, you reach a stage at which you are able to process things faster, and even at a subconscious level.

11 Counters Against Punches Using Kicks

Theoretically, using a kick to defend against a punch should be one of the safest ways of countering a technique – a kick should have a reach advantage over a punch as the legs are normally longer than the arms. That said, would a world-class boxer necessarily out-punch a world-class kicker? If the kicker could keep the puncher at bay with his legs, this could result in a victory for the kicker; however, if the puncher can get inside the kicker's legs, then the puncher could well be victorious.

There is much debate in the fighting world as to which art or discipline would come out on top should they all meet. Perhaps the answer is that ultimately it is down to the individual studying that art form or discipline.

The following drills will help you learn how to counter a punch using kicks as the weapon of choice. Various counter-strike methods and options are given for each punch.

Counters Against the Jab

The jab is an incredibly fast technique used primarily for probing through and opening up the guard, and of course for setting up that big powerful knockout punch. As such, when defending against a jab you need to be fast and very much alert, otherwise a skilled puncher will be more than likely to find his mark first.

Drill 1 – Lean-Back and Counter

The range for this one does not matter too much as you create the distance you need to kick by using the lean-back evasion; you do not necessarily need to stand at the kicking range. Be careful when getting in too close to your opponent, though, particularly if he is a good puncher. You are at even more risk if your speciality is mainly kicking and you could find yourself getting unstuck when you are

too close, as they will be more likely to beat you to the mark every time.

Ideally, when attempting to counter-fight a puncher using your kicks, you will need to stay more within the punching range, simply to entice your opponent to punch. Unless he can cover distance very quickly using his footwork (and never underestimate your opponent, particularly as the vast majority of punchers are more than capable of doing this), your standing mainly in the kicking range will lead to more of a distance fight than a counter-striking fight.

Fig 388 Lean back to evade the jab.

141

Fig 389 Front kick to the body to counter.

Fig 390 Lean back, transferring your weight on to your back foot.

As your opponent attempts to jab, transfer your body weight on to your back foot, leaning back and out of the way of the attack at the same time (Fig 388). As he commits to the punch he will expose his mid line and it is here that the transfer of weight to the back foot will enable you to stab out a lead-leg front kick to the left side of his body (Fig 389).

Drill 2 – Lean-Back and Counter, Version 2

This time, as your opponent attacks, lean back, transferring your body weight on to your rear foot (Fig 390). As you do, pivot slightly on your rear foot and round kick to the other side of the body (attacking the right side) (Fig 391). The transfer of body weight to the rear foot enables you to bring the lead leg off the floor much faster, without needing to adjust your body weight in order to counter-balance yourself. This in turn ensures you can kick much more quickly, which is of the utmost importance when countering a puncher.

Fig 391 Round kick to the body to counter.

Fig 392 Lean out of the way of the jab.

Fig 393 Hook kick over the outstretched arm to counter.

Drill 3 – Lean-Back and Counter, Version 3

This counter requires a considerable degree of flexibility and timing as you are looking to counter the punch as the opponent throws it; in the previous two drills, you wait until the punch is on its way before countering it.

With both of you in a left fighting stance, wait until your opponent commits to the attack and execute a hooking kick over his lead arm (the one that he should be punching with), so that the kick lands as the punch is at full extension. In executing the hook kick, you should automatically lean out of the way of the punch so, if your timing is good, you should find that starting your counter at the same time as your opponent attacks gives you a greater chance of landing your counterattack. Obviously this works slightly differently if your opponent fights in a right lead. Figs 392 and 393 show this drill in action.

Drill 4 – Lean-Back and Counter, Version 4

This drill uses the side kick as the counter-striking tool and works well if you find yourself in more of a side or angled stance. These two stances also work quite well against a puncher as the side of the arm and leg acts as a natural barrier against an attack and limits the target area available to your opponent. They also allow you to get your head out of the way more quickly, and ensure that you do not make the mistake of sticking your head out in front, which can sometimes happen when fighting in a front-on stance.

As your opponent commits to his attack, lean back out of the way (Fig 394). At the same time, push off with your lead leg in order to create the gap you need and stab out a side kick to the mid line, which should now be exposed (Fig 395).

Drill 5 – Lean-Back and Counter, Version 5

This counter-strike is a great one to do when your opponent exposes their mid line. The twisting motion that forms the basis of this kick automatically takes you out of range of the punch and perfectly sets up a back kick. Although you are still utilizing the lean-back evasion for this one, it is

143

Fig 394 Lean back out of the way of the attack.

Fig 395 Side kick to the body to counter.

actually more of a lean and twist. As with the hooking-kick counter, timing is crucial; you need to ensure that you have completed the spin and executed the kick at the point where the opponent's punch is at full extension. Any hesitation will mean that you lose that window of opportunity as your opponent will retract his punch and more than likely execute a second one while you are in mid-spin.

As he commits to his attack, lean back out of the way (Fig 396), twisting at the same time and delivering a spinning back kick to the now-exposed area of the mid line (Fig 397). The head and even the body are now a considerable distance away from the punch and yet the kick lands solidly.

Drill 6 – Jump-Back Evasion and Counter

This counter is named the 'jump-back evasion' as opposed to the 'lean-back evasion', to help you understand the exact motion required for it to work. It works extremely well should the opponent rush you.

In certain situations you do not have the time to retreat using footwork, particularly if your weight distribution at that moment is not quite right. You should find that, with practice, a jump backwards means you can evade the attack much more quickly, and at the same time create enough distance with which to kick. This jump-back evasion, coupled with a jumping side kick, incorporates the best of both and forms a great defensive manoeuvre.

As your opponent attacks, transfer your body weight on to your back foot, but bring your lead leg up into the air at the same time (Fig 398). From here, use the momentum of bringing the leg up to hop off your rear leg and project yourself backwards. As you travel backwards in the air, stab the side kick out while your opponent advances. If you do it correctly, you should find that, not only do you avoid the attack completely, but also, if your timing is right, your kick lands at the same time (Fig 399).

Fig 396 Lean out of the way of the jab.

Fig 397 Use a spinning back kick to the body to counter.

Fig 398 Bring your lead leg off the floor.

Fig 399 Jump back and stab out a side kick at the same time.

Fig 400 Lean back to evade the cross.

Fig 401 Front kick to the exposed area.

Fig 402 Zone out with the lead leg.

Fig 403 Round kick to the body to counter.

Counters Against the Cross

The cross punch can be used on its own but is often used in combination with the jab. The thought process behind the jab-cross combination is that the cross, which travels off the rear hand, needs to cover more distance before it lands. As a result of this, it can often be seen coming. The jab is nearer to the opponent and is therefore quicker. The downside with the jab is that it is not considered to be a knockout punch (although it can be in the right hands), whereas the cross, which has more time to build up momentum, can have a greater effect when it lands.

When training the following drills, isolate the cross at first and then, when you become more experienced with them, try adding in a jab and a cross, and dealing with both punches before you counter the last one.

Drill 1 – Lean-Back and Counter
With both of you in a left fighting stance, lean back to avoid the punch as the cross comes in (Fig 400).

From here, send a rear-leg front kick straight out to the opponent's mid line as this area is exposed (Fig 401).

Drill 2 – Zone and Counter
As your opponent throws his cross punch, zone out with the lead leg to avoid the attack, sending the punch over your rear shoulder and exposing the mid line once again (Fig 402). From here, send out a rear-leg round kick to the exposed area (Fig 403).

Drill 3 – Lean-Back and Counter, Version 2
As your opponent commits to the cross punch, lean back to avoid the initial impact of the punch and start the twisting motion for the jumping back kick (Fig 404). From here, jump and complete the twist, putting you out of reach of the punch, and stab out a back kick to the now-exposed mid line (Fig 405).

Fig 404 Lean back and twist at the same time.

Fig 405 Jumping back kick to counter the attack.

Fig 406 Lean back to avoid the punch.

Fig 407 Round kick to the head to counter.

Drill 4 – Lean-Back and Counter, Version 3

As the cross punch comes in, lean back slightly to avoid it (Fig 406) and use the lean to send a round kick up to the head of your opponent (Fig 407). As you attempt this counter, you might find that the shoulder of your opponent's rear (punching) arm acts as a natural barrier against your kick. For that reason it might be worth using the ball of the foot as the striking tool for the kick, as the few extra inches should almost guarantee the kick lands.

Drill 5 – Lean-Back and Counter, Version 4

This is for the more advanced student, as the jumping spinning hook kick is quite a difficult kick to perform anyway, without the added complication of having to get your distance and timing right in order to land it. An alternative to this kick could be the spinning hook kick, although your opponent's rear (punching) arm will act as a natural barrier against your kick. Ideally, for this type of kick to work, you need your partner to be in an opposite lead to you.

The jumping version of the spinning hooking kick is a good option because, if your opponent is fighting in the same lead as you, the height you gain from the jump should be enough to clear his arm. This in turn gets around the fact that it could get in the way and prevent your kick from landing.

As your opponent punches, lean back to evade the attack and at the same time start twisting your body in a clockwise motion to set up the jump and spin (Fig 408). From here, immediately jump into the air and drive your rear leg around using the momentum of the spin to generate the power and energy to bring the leg back round again (Fig 409).

Many of these drills use a lean-back evasion as a way of avoiding the attack. This has been done simply because of distance. In order to use a kick successfully as a counter-attack, you need to make sure you have the room to pull it off. Staying in close enough to block, parry or cover a punch means that you also run the risk of being in too close to kick.

Fig 408 Lean back to avoid the kick.

Fig 409 Perform a jumping spinning hook kick to counter the attack.

Counters Against the Hook

The hooking punch is known for being a close-range punch. This particular technique is designed for fighting in areas where even the straight punches (the jab and the cross) would be too awkward to use. For that reason, countering a hooking punch with a kick is no easy feat. If you are in close enough for your opponent to consider using a hooking punch, then you certainly need to understand body mechanics in order to pull off a successful counterstrike using a kick. There are a number of ways, however, that you can use kicks as a counter method against some close-range attacks.

Drill 1 – Lean-Back and Counter

From close range, with both of you in a left lead, lean back out of the way of the attack as your opponent performs a lead hooking punch (Fig 410). From here, use the leaning motion to drive a front-leg round kick up to the head of your opponent (Fig 411). It is highly likely that your opponent will be covering his body with his rear

arm, which is why you do not target this area, even though that would be the easier option. In addition, if you are close enough to your opponent to warrant them using a hooking punch, attempting to kick their mid line using your instep or ball might result in the kick missing completely, as it travels past their mid line and you make contact with your knee or thigh instead.

Instead, the distance created when you lean, and the angle of travel with the kick mean that, if the target is available, you are more likely to land a successful counter to the head than to the body.

Drill 2 – Lean-Back and Counter, Version 2

This one works along the same lines as the previous one except that you are now twisting the body and using a spinning hook kick to counter with. As your opponent hooks, lean back and at the same time twist your body in a clockwise direction,

149

Fig 410 Lean back to avoid the hooking punch.

Fig 411 Round kick to the head of your opponent.

Fig 412 Lean back to evade the hook and start to spin.

Fig 413 Counter with a spinning hook kick.

driving your rear shoulder round to set up the kick (Fig 412). As you twist, send a rear-leg spinning hook kick up to the head of your opponent to finish the attack (Fig 413).

You need to ensure your distance is correct, otherwise you are more likely to connect with your calf muscle than your foot, due to being in too close. If, as you lean, you feel you are too close to spin, either change the counter-attack completely or simply step across slightly with your lead foot to change your body position. A bit of time invested in this drill will help you understand how to adjust your footing to get the best out of the counter.

This is another example of a kick that requires timing in order to pull it off. Because there is a spin involved, it is going to be slower than a static kick performed off the spot. Even if you are lightning fast, the chances are that your opponent is still going to have time to execute and retract his attack before you have had a chance to land yours. For this reason, you need to start the kick the second your opponent starts his attack and trust that the spinning motion will be enough to prevent the punch from landing, and that you have timed it correctly so that your opponent has no time to change his attack as yours comes round.

Drill 3 – Rolling Evasion and Counter

As your opponent throws the lead hooking punch, drop down and roll underneath it, moving from left to right (Figs 414 and 415). From here, you can kick to the body, if this target is available (Fig 416). Alternatively, using more of an angular round kick (*see* page 152), bring the leg up and through the centre of the guard, attacking the head instead (Fig 417).

Counters Against the Uppercut

Kicks may also be used to defend and counter against an uppercut attack. Because of the way it travels, the uppercut can be a very effective attack and also very difficult to defend. If the guard is not really tight there is a good chance that the punch, if used properly, will find a way through. Bringing yourself too far into the fight will make a counter-kick very difficult, so you need to continue with the lean-back evasion and look at using kicks to counter-strike with that work well against an uppercut.

Fig 414 Drop to evade the hook.

Fig 415 Roll under the punch.

Fig 416 Round kick to the body.

Fig 417 Use an angular round kick to attack the head.

Fig 418 Lean back to avoid the uppercut.

Fig 419 Axe kick to counter.

Drill 1 – Lean-Back and Counter

As your opponent attacks, lean back and, as you do, use the energy of the lean to generate enough momentum to swing the lead leg up, over the opponent's punching arm and drive an axe kick down, targeting the head (Figs 418 and 419). This is quite a difficult movement and requires some flexibility in order to pull off, but it is worth persevering with – the axe kick is a great kick, which, if done properly, not only adds its own natural defence to the attack but can be very difficult to defend against.

Drill 2 – Zone and Counter

A zone defence will give you something different to work with. It does take you out of the range of your opponent's attack, but it can be quite a slow method of defence. That is not to say that it is ineffective, just that you need to ensure you do not pause for too long in between the movement and the counter, thereby giving your opponent time either to recover or throw a second technique.

Working from a left lead (Fig 420), step out at a 45-degree angle with your lead leg when the attack comes in (Fig 421). At the same time, and to reduce the delay, chamber the leg and send out a rear-leg side kick to the mid line of your opponent (Fig 422).

Drill 3 – Lean-Back and Counter, Version 2

This drill utilizes the lean-back principles to counter-attack using a round kick as the striking weapon.

As the attack comes in, evade it by leaning back out of the way, at the same time transferring your body weight on to your back foot, thereby allowing your lead leg to come off the floor (Fig 423).

Fig 421 Zone out with your lead leg to evade the uppercut.

Fig 420 In your left lead.

Fig 422 Side kick to the body to counter the attack.

At the same time, use the energy of the lean-back evasion to bring your kicking leg up and target the head of your opponent using a round kick (Fig 424). If your opponent is a little sloppy with his guard, you should be able to get away with using the instep as the striking tool; if his guard is quite tight, you may need to use the ball of the foot instead. Just be sure to pivot slightly on your rear leg to ensure your body is in the correct position for the hips to open correctly.

Self-Development

These drills should be enough to keep you going for some time and it is recommended that you work methodically through one section at a time, before moving on to the next. It would be easy enough to put together a whole load of drills utilizing every defence and every possible kick, but this could be quite inhibiting to your training. Instead, work through the drills given here until you can competently perform the counter-strikes against the suggested attacks. Then you can try adding in additional counters of your own, working from varying angles and positions, using your natural ability at each stage in order to improve your skill at countering an attack using your kicks.

Much of martial arts study is about self-development. The key to physical self-development in this case is having the ability to take what you have been shown and adapt it so that it works for you. All the drills given here are designed to stretch you in various ways, to help you step outside your comfort zone and understand that you can push yourself as far as you want (providing of course that you do actually want to push yourself). Once you realize this, then you will also realize that you yourself are the only limitation on what you can do.

As you become increasingly proficient with the drills described here, you will naturally start to come up with your own. This is all part of that development process and a natural part of your evolution. However, you do need to understand the basics of each drill before you can do this, otherwise you run the risk of weakening your foundations, which are the key to everything you do.

Fig 423 Lean back to avoid the uppercut.

Fig 424 Round kick to the head to counter the attack.

12 Counters Against Kicks Using Kicks

Countering a kick with a kick is possibly the most difficult counter-attack of all. If two like-minded, identically matched kickers face off, which one is likely to win? In reality, many elements will need to be taken into account in order to theorize the outcome, and it is purely hypothetical, since the chance of you actually meeting someone identically matched is pretty slim. In competitive fighting, the stats of two fighters may well look identical on paper, but in the majority of competitive fights there is always a winner and a loser (although, occasionally, fighters may draw). The winner on a particular occasion will simply be the one who fights better on the day.

Although it is difficult, there is always a way of defending a kick from a competent kicker, and of determining the most effective way to return the attack using a kick. The following drills will show you how.

Fig 425 Face your opponent in a left lead.

Counters Against the Front Kick

There are three basic kicks that anyone studying one of the kicking arts will inevitably learn first: the front kick, the round kick (also known as the roundhouse kick in karate or the turning kick in taekwon-do) and the side kick. Of these three kicks, the round kick is probably used the most, closely followed by the front kick for full-contact fighting or the side kick for light continuous fighting.

The front kick can be a very fast and versatile kick, used just as effectively off the lead leg as the rear leg. When dealing with a straight-line kick such as this, it is never really advisable to move backwards as a good kicker will still land the kick. Instead, try veering off to the side so the kick travels past you. This is where you can set up your counter-strike.

Fig 426 Zone right to evade the kick.

Fig 427 Counter with a lead-leg round kick.

Fig 428 Face your opponent.

Fig 429 Zone left as the kick comes on.

Fig 430 Side kick to the mid line of your opponent.

Timing

It is worth noting that, in order to perform a successful counter-strike against a kicker, your timing needs to be spot on. The most effective time to counter a kick with a kick is when the opponent is committing to an attack or is caught off balance. This is generally when he is retracting his kick with a view to either landing the leg or when he is chambering it for a second attack.

If your timing is good then there is a high probability that your counter-attack will land. However, if you mistime it, there is also a high probability that your counter will fall short and you then run the risk of getting caught with a follow-up shot.

Drill 1 – Zone and Counter

With both fighters in a left lead (Fig 425), the opponent thrusts out a rear-leg front kick. As he does this, zone out with the right leg so the kick travels past (Fig 426). As the opponent retracts the kick and starts to land the leg, fire out a lead-leg round kick to the body (Fig 427).

Drill 2 – Zone and Counter, Version 2

From your fighting stance (Fig 428), zone out

with the left leg as the opponent thrusts out a lead-leg front kick (Fig 429). From here, perform a rear-leg side kick to the mid line as the opponent lands his leg (Fig 430).

Fig 432 Spin step to avoid the kick.

Fig 431 Square off against your opponent.

Fig 433 Front kick to the body to counter.

Drill 3 – Spin Step and Counter

This final drill counters a front kick with a front kick. So far, all the counter-strikes have been to the mid-section of your opponent, but if this target area is not available, you should consider taking the kicks up to the head. Both of you face off in a left lead (Fig 431). As your opponent steps up to front kick, spin off in a clockwise direction using your rear leg – keep your lead leg where it is and push off with your rear leg in a clockwise direction (Fig 432). From here, thrust out a lead-leg front kick to the open target area your opponent gives you (Fig 433).

Counters Against the Round Kick

This time the angle of attack is changed, using a round kick and the side of the body is targeted instead of the front. The round kick is a very dangerous kick as it can be used to target the legs (inner and outer thigh region in particular), the mid line and the head, making it incredibly versatile too. The only downside with the round kick is that, because it travels in a circular motion, it can be quite easy to defend against.

Drill 1 – Cover and Counter

This defence works well against a round kick providing your timing is good, as you rely on the opponent's attempt to recover from his attack to

Fig 435 Use a single-arm defence to block the kick.

Fig 434 Face your opponent.

Fig 436 Counter with a round kick as the opponent retracts his leg.

your advantage. In a left lead (Fig 434), cover your head using a single-arm cover as your opponent kicks (Fig 435). As he starts to retract his leg, use speed and timing to shoot out a lead-leg round

kick to the head or body (depending on which is the most vulnerable), taking advantage of his poor position as he attempts to recover from his kick (Fig 436).

Drill 2 – Parry and Counter

This counter works well with the parry but is slightly more advanced, due to the spin. Just make sure your kicking ability is good enough to pull this off under pressure; if not, it might be worth while investing a little time practising it before attempting it for real. With you both in a left lead (Fig 437), parry your opponent's attempt to round kick with your lead hand and, as you do, turn your body into the defence in preparation for the spin (Fig 438). As your opponent attempts to recover from his attack, continue to turn and land a spinning hook kick or reverse round kick to the head (or body if the head is covered) (Fig 439).

Drill 3 – Shin Block and Counter

This simple defence is probably the most effective method of blocking a low-level round kick to the leg. If your flexibility allows, you can also use the shin block to defend against a kick to the body. Just be careful with straight kicks such as the side

Fig 437 Face your opponent.

Fig 438 Parry the round kick with your lead hand.

Fig 439 Counter with a spinning hook kick.

Fig 440 Face your opponent.

Fig 441 Shin block the round kick attack.

Fig 442 Without landing your leg, thrust out a front kick to the mid line.

kick or spinning back kick, as they are very powerful. If your balance is not great, even though you may well block the attack, you are more than likely going to find yourself on the floor.

Square off with your opponent (Fig 440). As your opponent attacks, stop the kick, using your shin. Remember to create a shield by connecting your forearm with the knee, just in case the kick rides up towards your face (Fig 441). As your opponent recovers from his attack, keep your leg where it is and fire out a front kick to his body (Fig 442).

Drill 4 – Parry and Counter, Version 2
This defence and counter works equally well using a jumping back kick as it does with the spinning version. In fact, the jumping version is both faster and more powerful.

In your fighting stance (Fig 443), parry a lead-leg round kick from your opponent (Fig 444). For this particular parry, it is advisable to use the forearm to defend the attack instead of the palm. The palm will work fine, but the forearm has a greater surface area, so, in the heat of the attack, it is more likely to be effective. As soon as you have stopped

Fig 443 Face your opponent.

Fig 444 Parry the round kick with your lead hand or forearm.

the kick, use the movement of the parry to counter-attack with a spinning back kick to the opponent's mid line (Fig 445).

Fig 445 Counter with a spinning back kick to the body.

Counters Against the Side Kick

The side kick is an extremely powerful attacking kick that also acts as a natural defence due to its position when striking. Even if it is blocked, it can still be quite difficult to counter as the kicking leg acts as a natural obstacle creating a barrier between you and your opponent. As such, it is worth considering a few alternative methods of countering an attack using this particular kick; the simple 'universal block' may stop the attack from landing, but make it very difficult to counter, especially if the opponent sends out two or three of the same kick simultaneously.

Drill 1 – Step-In Defence and Counter

Face your opponent in the same lead (Fig 446). As you see your opponent begin his attack, step in close, in order to close the gap and at the same time prevent him from having enough room to extend the kick fully. Be sure to keep your guard tight in case he follows with a punch, as you are now in the punching range (Fig 447). From here, use the step-in motion to counter with a close-range axe kick across your opponent's blind side (Fig 448).

161

Fig 446 Face your opponent.

Look for signs of your opponent telegraphing the attack, such as a step up with the back foot. This is generally done to reposition the back leg and offer support to the body as the front leg comes off the floor.

Drill 2 – React and Counter

With this counter you use to your advantage speed, timing and the possibility of your opponent not guarding himself properly as he kicks. In your fighting stance (Fig 449), as soon as you see your opponent begin his attack, beat him to the kick, attacking the mid-line gap that is naturally created by him not protecting himself properly (Fig 450).

The key to the success of this counter is to ensure that you are already primed and ready to fire out that side kick as soon as your opponent commits to his attack. In reality, you probably need to know that you are going to kick before your opponent gives away what he is planning to do, as you need to be in position prior to your opponent attacking. With this counter you would send out a side kick,

Fig 447 Step in to absorb the kick.

Fig 448 Counter with an axe kick using the lead leg.

Fig 449 Face off against your opponent.

Fig 450 Sneak a side kick into the gap as your opponent kicks.

regardless of the attack with which your opponent leads. The skill of course is in guiding your kick, at speed, into the gap that your opponent creates as he attacks.

The Blind Side

The blind side is the side that your opponent leads with. For example, if your opponent fights with his left side predominantly in front, then this is his blind side. It is referred to as the blind side because the shoulder that is in front naturally obstructs the peripheral vision (the ability to see all around without the need to focus on something) on the left side, thereby making an attack that originates from this side of the body much more difficult to see coming.

Try a little experiment to prove this point. Instruct your partner to stand in his fighting stance and note which leg he places in front (for the purposes of this example, the left one). Now stand in very close, so that your chest almost touches his forward shoulder, and place your hands by your side. Bring your left hand towards his face and ask him to tell you when he can see it. Now repeat the exercise with your right arm and note how much closer you can get your hand to his face before he sees it.

Fig 451 Face your opponent.

Fig 452 Lean back so the attack falls short.

Fig 453 Counter with a hop-step hook kick.

Fig 454 Face your opponent.

Fig 455 Lean back out of the way of the hook kick.

Fig 456 Round kick to the body to counter.

Drill 3 – Lean-Back and Counter
This time with both of you in the same lead (Fig 451), as your partner steps in to side kick, lean back out of the way so the kick falls short (Fig 452). As your opponent retracts his leg, step or hop in and hook kick to the head as he is recovering (Fig 453).

Counters Against the Hook Kick

The hook kick is quite an underused attacking kick, making way for the more commonly seen axe kick instead. The following four drills show some simple moves that can be used as effective defence and counters against a hooking-kick attack.

Drill 1 – Lean-Back and Counter
With both you and your opponent in a left lead (Fig 454), wait until the hooking kick comes in and, by transferring your body weight on to your rear leg, lean out of the way of the attack (Fig 455). As the kick travels past your head, fire out a lead-leg round kick to the body (Fig 456).

Fig 457 Face your opponent in a left lead.

Fig 458 Lean back to evade the attack.

Fig 459 Round kick to counter as the opponent retracts their attack.

Fig 460 In a left lead.

Drill 2 – Lean-Back and Counter, Version 2

As before, the same defence and counter for this attack will also work quite effectively to the head. This is due to the fact that the hook kick from your opponent will pass across your body, putting him off balance as he begins to recover and opening up his body slightly as the kick passes to the opposite side. A counter-strike to the inside of his body at this point is likely to be more effective than attempting to attack the opposite side (using a hooking-kick counter as an example). Figs 457 to 459 show this counter in action.

Drill 3 – Step-In and Counter

In a left lead (Fig 460), step in to absorb the attack as soon as you see your opponent telegraph this kick (Fig 461). You should now be in too close for his kick to land (in fact, the striking part of the foot should now pass harmlessly behind you) and your forward movement should put your opponent off balance. As he recovers from this defence, send a hooking kick of your own up to the head to counter (Fig 462).

Fig 461 Step in to absorb the attack.

Fig 462 Hook kick to counter the attack.

Fig 463 In a fighting stance.

Fig 464 Drop to evade the kick.

Fig 465 Roll underneath the leg.

Fig 466 Side kick to the mid line of your opponent.

Fig 467 Face your opponent.

Drill 4 – Rolling Evasion and Counter

From your fighting stance (Fig 463), turn away from the kick and start to roll as your opponent starts his attack (Fig 464). As the kick passes over your head, use your body mechanics to take you underneath his leg (Fig 465) and send out a rear-leg side kick to the mid line as your opponent attempts to recover (Fig 466).

Counters Against the Axe Kick

The axe kick is the last static kick to consider before finishing on some advanced kicking defence and counter drills. In many cases, inexperienced fighters will panic when an axe kick comes towards them and, instead of moving the head out of the way (if they do not have time to block it), will attempt to duck. This is the worst thing to do against a descending attack as the axe kick will simply hit on its way down. The following drills are simple yet effective for countering against an axe-kick attack using your kicks.

Fig 468 Lean back to avoid the axe kick.

Fig 469 Hook kick to the head as your opponent recovers.

Fig 470 Face your opponent.

Drill 1 – Lean-Back and Counter

In a left lead (Fig 467), transfer your body weight on to your rear leg and lean back (not to the side) as the axe kicks comes in (Fig 468). If done properly, the kick should pass in front of you and, providing your opponent does not use the axe kick to set up a second attack, you can send out a lead-leg hook kick to the head as he lands his leg (Fig 469).

The beauty with this one is that, as soon as you have avoided the axe kick, your body weight should naturally be on the back foot, allowing you to bring your lead leg straight up for a counter-strike. If you are too far away at this stage, simply hop in to cover the distance so that the kick can find its mark.

Drill 2 – Step-In and Counter

The final drill for the static kicks uses the step-in defence at its best. This simple defence can be effective against the vast majority of kicks, but it works exceptionally well with an axe kick. One possibility of this defence is that your opponent's leg

Fig 471 Step in to absorb the kick.

Fig 472 Return the attack with an axe kick counter.

Counters Against the Spinning Hook Kick

This kick requires incredible speed and timing in order to pull it off successfully in sparring or a competitive bout, and it also opens the kicker up to many a counter-attack. For these reasons, you only really see it being performed by inexperienced fighters (who do not yet realize that they should not be doing them) or advanced kickers with highly developed abilities. However, you do need to be aware of ways in which to defend against it.

Drill 1 – Lean-Back and Counter
With both of you in the same lead (Fig 473), transfer your body weight on to your back leg as your opponent turns his back to start the spin (Fig 474). As the kick comes round, simply lean out of the way so it passes overhead (Fig 475). At this point, fire out a lead-leg side kick to the open body as your opponent tries to land the leg back round (Fig 476).

Once he has committed to this kick, it can be very difficult for the opponent to pull out of it. As becomes trapped on your shoulder, allowing you to counter his attack effectively (with a punch), without there being much he can do about it.

Alternatively, a simple step forwards at this point will send your opponent to the mats, which of course will buy you a valuable few seconds of recovery and tire him out even more as he now needs to climb back up off the floor. There is also a psychological element that comes into play when someone gets knocked over; anyone who has ever found himself on the floor during a stand-up bout will know how demoralizing it can be.

In a left lead (Fig 470), look for the tell-tale, telegraphing signs of an axe kick (there is likely to be a step-up that will occur before the kick) and, as you see the leg rise, step in close to absorb the attack (Fig 471). Make sure you are quick with this defence as the axe kick can be a very fast kick if done properly; if you hesitate, there is a good chance the kick will land. As your opponent begins his recovery, centre your balance and send a lead-leg axe kick back to counter (Fig 472).

Fig 473 Face off against your opponent.

Fig 474 Transfer your body weight on to your rear leg.

Fig 475 Lean out of the way of the kick.

Fig 476 Side kick to counter.

a result, if you can avoid his kick completely, there is a high probability that you can time your attack just right and land a counter-strike as he is attempting to recover.

Drill 2 – React and Counter

This counter is another sneaky one that takes advantage of the fact that your opponent has had to turn his back. In a left lead (Fig 477), fire out a lead-leg side kick to the mid line as soon as your opponent starts the spin, sending him off balance (Fig 478).

There is a chance with this one that you may be a little premature and instead catch the back with your side kick. If the back scores in the rules you fight to, this is of course fine; if not, the only advantage you will gain here is the same as described for the axe kick. Ideally, try to catch your opponent in the side (under the arm) if you can, as you should still gain the point (with an observant referee), and if you do then knock them over, you get the bonus of the psychological victory as well.

Fig 477 Face your opponent in a left lead.

Fig 478 Send out a side kick as your opponent starts to spin.

Fig 479 Face your opponent.

Fig 480 Lean back to evade the spinning kick.

Fig 481 Fire out a round kick as your opponent spins out of the kick.

Drill 3 – Lean-Back and Counter

This final drill takes on a similar theme to the first one with the only difference being the counter-strike. In a left lead (Fig 479), lean back as your opponent spins (Fig 480). As the kick travels past your head, fire out a lead-leg round kick to the head

(or body, depending on which is open at the time) as your opponent attempts to recover (Fig 481).

Working Through the Drills

Be sure to work methodically through the drills, starting at the beginning and moving on only when you feel you have reached a level at which you can successfully pull off the drill in a realistic situation.

There is no need to include every kick, every defence and every possible counter here. By this stage in your training, you should have recognized that the principles of defending and even countering an attack remain the same, regardless of the technique against which you are defending. It is up to you to take the principles and elements contained within the drills you have studied so far, and adapt them so that they work for you against all the kicks and punches you are likely to encounter.

It does not matter how good you are or how many black belts you may have, when you spar for real you are going to get hit. Knife combat experts say that, no matter how good you may be at defending against a blade, if a knife is drawn in combat, you are going to get cut before you win the fight. The same is true in terms of getting hit in sparring. Respect this and use the knowledge to your advantage. When you do try a defence that does not work, have the humility, attitude and ability to reset and try again.

13 Continuous Sparring

There are two types of sparring within kickboxing: continuous sparring and point sparring. A continuous fight is conducted over a set time period, somewhere between two and five minutes on average. During this time, the two fighters will fight continuously, aiming to land as many legal kicks and punches to the scoring zones on the opponent's body as possible. To help keep track of the number of clean shots that land there will be a number of corner referees or judges (they both do the same job but are sometimes referred to by different names). Each referee will have a pair of counters or, if they are using the old-fashioned method, a pen and paper, and their job is to keep a score of each point gained by each fighter. At the end of the bout the main referee (the one in the middle with the two fighters) will ask for the judges' scores and the fighter who has gained the most points will get the decision.

Although there are, of course, slight variations, this is generally how it works. Within the competitive world of continuous sparring you will also find full-contact bouts and light-contact bouts. In full contact, the two fighters hit each other as hard as they can, aiming to inflict as much damage as possible on their opponent, and ultimately finishing the fight before the end of the round. This can be done through a knockout (KO), which is generally awarded when the opponent is unable to continue fighting due to unconsciousness, injury or fatigue. The variation on the knockout is the technical knockout (TKO), when the fight is stopped by the referee, the ring doctor or the fighter's corner men (by throwing in the towel, for example) deciding that it is in the best interest of one fighter to stop fighting.

Light continuous bouts do not use the knockout or technical knockout rule as, theoretically, they should not need them. Light continuous involves continuous fighting for the full duration of the bout (except in the case of injury, fatigue or accidental knockout), reducing the power of each technique so that only a light blow is made to the opponent. This form of continuous fighting is by far the safer method and one highly recommended for anyone new to the world of sparring. It also demands greater control, since it is easy for light continuous bouts to end up as full-contact bouts if the fighters are unable to restrain their attacks. This is where a good referee comes in. His job is not only to consider the welfare of the fighters but also to ensure that neither fighter gets too carried away with their power.

In full-contact events, fighters tend to focus more on their punching ability and use only the basic kicks such as the front kick and the round kick. Flashier kicks, such as the spinning, jumping and jumping spinning ones, are used less often, as they require much more energy to perform. As full-contact fighting is one of the most physically demanding styles of fighting, the experienced fighter will prefer to conserve as much energy as he can throughout the fight. Instead, he will use only the most basic of attacks rather than those more draining techniques that, due to the incredible degree of speed and timing required in order to pull them off, will not only deplete their energy banks a lot faster, but are also much harder to land.

Light continuous bouts will often incorporate flashier techniques, with top-level fighters performing multiple kicks as well as spinning, jumping and jumping spinning kicks. Although these types of kicks are still physically demanding, because the emphasis is now on only touching the opponent as opposed to breaking them down, less power is required and less energy is used. The other great advantage is that you are definitely not as sore the next day after competing in a light contact event as you are after competing in a full-contact event!

The following simple drills are designed for the competitive fighter, divided into beginner, intermediate and advanced levels, and can be used for either full- or light-contact fighting. With all of these combinations it is very easy simply to string together a load of techniques and call it a drill. Instead, the combinations given here work well together and it will be beneficial for you to consider the reasons why they work better than other combinations you might see. As with everything, your main job is to study as much as you can and then determine what works best for you, leaving out what does not.

Beginner Level Drills

Many fighters fail to understand the various angles of attack that can be used when fighting. If you adopt a traditional kick-and-punch approach to fighting, you will find that a tight guard from your opponent covers most of the attacks you send his way. For that reason you need to focus

more on the various striking parts that can be used when kicking, and the direction of travel for the various kicks available to you.

Note: for the following drills I have chosen to remove my protective sparring equipment so that you can clearly see the foot position when attacking. You are not advised to do this when you train these drills for real, as the risk of injury to both you and your partner is greatly increased.

Round Kicks

Traditional Round Kick High Section
If you use a traditional round kick to attack when striking with the instep, the attack is relatively easy to defend against (*see* Fig 482). Your opponent has only to keep the guard where it naturally should be to protect the head safely from this attack.

Traditional Round Kick Variation
Changing the striking part of the foot will enable you to utilize the kick more effectively. Now,

Fig 482 Round kick using the instep.

Fig 483 Round kick using the ball of the foot.

Fig 484 Mid-section round kick using the instep.

Fig 485 Mid-section round kick using the ball of the foot.

instead of attacking with the instep, pull the foot back and strike using the ball of the foot (be sure to pull your toes back so you do not catch them as the kick connects). If done correctly, the foot should bend around the opponent's guard and you should hit your target solidly with the ball of the foot (Fig 483).

It is important to use this striking tool in the right environment and with extreme control. You are hitting your opponent with an area of your foot that is not covered, thereby offering no protection to your partner.

Traditional Round Kick To The Body

As with the last attack, a traditional round kick to the body can be easily blocked with little or no effort from your opponent, providing his guard is held where it should be. In this example the defender has chosen to use more of a universal-style block to defend against this kick; clearly, it is the rear arm that actually blocks the attack and the lead arm is purely used as extra cover (Fig 484).

Traditional Round Kick Variation

Changing the striking tool from the instep to the ball of the foot instantly allows the foot to penetrate the guard and 'sneak' into the gap naturally created by holding the arms in this position. Even the tightest of universal defences have trouble covering all areas so, with a little time spent developing your targeting ability, you should have no trouble at all finding a gap for the foot to land (Fig 485).

Angular Round Kick to the Head

The previous two drills involved using a traditional-style round kick (with a circular motion of travel), changing the striking tool to a much smaller and more penetrating part of the foot. The leg still moves in the same way, but the difference between it finding its mark and simply bouncing off the guard is the foot position.

In this drill you will not only change the striking tool but also go against tradition and change the line of travel. Now, as your opponent holds his arms in the same manner as before, utilizing more of a front-on defence, you bring the leg straight up off the floor, aiming to kick in between his guard, striking the head (or chin in this case) from a different angle (Fig 486).

If you think of the kick now as more of a hybrid front kick crossed with a round kick, this will probably help you to understand exactly how the leg moves. If done properly you will greatly increase your chances of striking the head and, where full contact is concerned, improve your chances of a knockout.

Angular Round Kick to the Body
The same line of travel works just as effectively to the body, in fact if your flexibility is not quite there yet, you may find this target area much more preferable with this angle of attack. From your fighting stance, wait until you see the lead hand move away from the body and target your kick to land underneath the arm. Look at the lead arm position of the defender in Fig 485; an angular round kick would not work, as your foot would simply bounce off the opponent's lead arm, and a circular attack using the ball of the foot would be more appropriate.

However, as your opponent brings his lead arm slightly away from his body – either because he is priming it ready to strike with or because everyone naturally moves their arms around when sparring – it presents you with a great opportunity to use the angular round kick (Fig 487).

Side Kicks

The Traditional Side Kick to the Body
The same tricks work well with a traditional side kick. Usually, students are taught to send a side kick out in a straight line, and it is often drilled in to them that, if the leg does not travel parallel to the floor, then most of the energy of the kick is lost. This is not strictly true, and in fact a side kick to the face can be very effective. Nevertheless, in kickboxing you are more likely to find a side kick used to attack the body than anywhere else.

As you chamber this kick (*see* Fig 488), you naturally set the leg up to travel straight out and, providing your opponent holds his guard tight in readiness to receive this kick, he will block it every time (Fig 489).

Fig 486 Angled round kick to the head using the ball of the foot.

Fig 487 Angled round kick to the body using the ball.

Fig 488 A traditional side kick in chambered position.

Fig 489 The traditional side kick hits the guard.

The Rising Side Kick

This drill goes against tradition and shows you how to perform a rising side kick that can penetrate all but the tightest of defences. As your opponent makes the mistake of bringing the lead arm away from the body, chamber your leg a little lower than before; in the example, this movement has been exaggerated so you can clearly see it, but the attack still works against the slightest movement (Fig 490).

From here, send the leg upwards instead of out, so that it knocks the opponent's lead arm out of the

Fig 490 A sparring side kick in chambered position.

Fig 491 The sparring side kick lands.

way as it connects with it. Then, once the arm is clear, simply stab the leg out so that it actually hits the target instead of just resting there (Fig 491). If you incorporate the rising side kick with a hop step (*see* pages 186–7) once the arm is clear – this takes some considerable timing to get right, but with a little training you should manage it – you can sneak the side kick in and also deliver some considerable power at the same time.

This simple technique has been known to break ribs, so *be careful*!

Beginner Combos

These simple combinations work well together in a continuous bout. The key thing to understand with continuous fighting is that your opponent is expecting to be attacked with several techniques, so if you send out just one at a time, the likelihood of that single technique landing is very slim. On the other hand, if you are fast enough to land a single shot, you are very likely then to receive five or six back.

It is often said that, if ten shots are thrown, the first few are blocked, the next few are evaded and the last few land. As a result, when fighting the continuous way, you need to get used to sending out a barrage of attacks with the intention of opening up your opponent in order to create weakness in his defence, enabling you to land the last few attacks – and landing them well.

The following combos work well as they are simple to perform but cause opponents to react in such a way that they open themselves up as they attempt to cover your opening attacks.

Beginner Combo 1

From your fighting stance send out a jab to the head. Your opponent should react by blocking it (Fig 492). To ensure that he keeps his guard in place, and to set you up for your final attack, send out a cross (Fig 493). From here, use the body position and energy of the cross to drive a rear round kick out to the area he has now exposed as a result of blocking your last two attacks (Fig 494).

Naturally, this is not foolproof and it is quite possible that your opponent could decide to slip the first attack, which would then throw the rest of the combo completely out. Your skill now comes in with the speed at which you can react to

Fig 492 Send out a jab to raise the guard ...

Fig 493 ... a cross.

Fig 494 Finish with a rear leg round kick to the exposed area.

Fig 495 Send out a lead leg axe kick ...

Fig 496 ... a cross to bring the guard to the front.

Fig 497 Finish with a lead hook to the exposed area.

this unexpected move and change your strategy, allowing you to recover and put together a new set of attacks based on how the fight has changed and to where your opponent has now moved. This ability to adapt is what makes the difference between an adequate fighter and a great fighter.

Beginner Combo 2

This time, create a different reaction in your opponent by sending out a lead-leg axe kick to the head (Fig 495). If it lands, you can continue with the combo, but if the first attack is evaded, you should use the energy of driving the kick down to send out a cross punch (Fig 496). As your opponent defends this second attack, send out a lead hook to the head, sneaking the punch through the window created in the side of his defence (Fig 497).

Practise the above drills, particularly the variations on the traditional kicks, using focus pads first. Ensure your partner can feed the pads well and understands exactly how to hold them to represent the body position realistically and the striking areas correctly.

Start off slowly at first, working correct technique and body mechanics and slowly introducing speed and power. Then, once you have mastered the drills using the pads, work them on your partner in the same way.

Intermediate Level Drills

At this level, you can start to introduce some multiple kicks into your training. The focus with the double kick is to use the initial kick to set up the second kick. Multiple kicking does require a good level of flexibility, balance and body mechanics and, if you consider yourself to be around the intermediate level but have not yet come across this style of kicking before, then a little time and effort invested here will pay off.

There are many fighters who lack the ability to kick well. They can throw a kick out easily enough and, by using pure momentum, even attack the head. However, the skill comes from being in control throughout every stage of the kick and not letting the kick control you. For example, you will often see fighters throw a kick out and then find

themselves off balance or open to a counter-attack because they have not developed their kicking ability to a high enough standard, and cannot actually control the kick throughout the full duration of the attack.

It is not just about sending the kick out. Great emphasis also needs to be put on the landing and recovery. Many fighters have trouble when faced with an experienced opponent as it is not difficult for participants of a high level to be able to work out their opponent within the first few attacks. Once your opponent realizes that you are not a great kicker, he will simply wait for you to kick and then use to his advantage your inability to control the kick through all its stages. Consequently it is worth spending some considerable time working the next few drills. Not only will it add another weapon to your arsenal, but it will also help you to develop many of the qualities and elements required to kick successfully.

The Double Round Kick Combo

This is a great set-up technique and is used to lure your opponent into lowering his guard, enabling you to strike to the exposed area of the head. In your fighting stance, send out a lead-leg round kick to the body (lead-leg kicks are usually much faster than rear-leg kicks). As your opponent sees the kick approaching, the natural reaction is to drop the guard slightly in order to block it (Fig 498). As soon as the kick lands, bounce it off the body, re-chamber it (Fig 499), and send it up to the head, striking with either the instep or the ball of the foot (Fig 500).

Although you cannot fully appreciate the speed required for this combination to work, the time between the first kick and the second kick needs to be as short as possible, otherwise your opponent will have enough time to bring his guard back up to defend against the second attack. One key tip with this combination is to keep the knee as high as possible. If you kick the body and then drop the knee slightly, you have to use up more time and energy bringing the knee back up to the original position. Ideally, the knee remains in pretty much the same position for the first kick as it does for the second kick (*see* Figs 498 to 500). You might even want to bring the knee up to the same level as you

Fig 498 Send out a lead-leg round kick to the body to bring the guard down.

Fig 499 Re-chamber the leg without landing it.

Fig 500 Strike to the exposed area with the second round kick.

would if starting out with a head kick, even though you are kicking to the body first.

The Round Kick–Side Kick Combo

This time, the aim is to open up the body but remain in the kicking range. One of the most effective ways to do this is to send out a lead-leg round kick to the head (Fig 501). As the kick is blocked, note where the other arm is, as your opponent might make the mistake of leaving his body unguarded; if he does, pull the leg back in and chamber it for a side kick (Fig 502), striking to the open area (Fig 503).

The Hook Kick–Round Kick Combo

This combination is designed to lead your opponent into a false sense of security and works particularly well against a counter-fighter. As you perform your lead-leg hook kick, the natural reaction for your opponent is to lean out of the way of the attack and let the kick sail past (Fig 504). (If he blocks it, as is quite possible, you will need to change tactics mid-flow; if he does not, you can continue as follows.)

Fig 501 Send out a round kick to the head to bring the guard up.

Fig 502 Re-chamber the leg for a side kick.

With an attack of this nature, your opponent may well assume that you are going to land your leg, giving him an ideal opportunity to explode in and counter while you are recovering. Instead, allow the leg to pass in front of your opponent but stop it mid-flow and re-chamber it (Fig 505). Then, if your timing is good, as your opponent moves in to counter, you can send a round kick

Fig 503 Kick to the exposed area.

Fig 504 Send out a lead-leg hook kick to the head.

Fig 505 Re-chamber the leg as your opponent attempts to counter.

Fig 506 Send out a round kick to the head.

back up to the head. There is a good chance that it will land (Fig 506).

Hop-Step Kicks

One of the beginner drills involves a hop-step side kick. The hop-step technique can help you to develop lightning-fast kicks that your opponent will not see coming, and this drill will show you how to do it.

One of the big mistakes that fighters make is to telegraph their techniques – that is to say, they perform some kind of pre-attack movement that gives away what they are about to do. For example, a puncher might use the roll of a shoulder or the slight drop of a hand to set up a punch; for the kicker, the most common telegraph is a simple step using the rear leg.

This pre-attack move generally relates either to covering distance or to the attacker having to adjust his stance, which is too long to support his body properly as he lifts his kicking leg off the floor. The problem here of course is that the experienced fighter will pick up on this movement and predict what is coming. Once he has made this prediction, he inevitably has a greater chance of

defending against the attack than if he had been caught unawares.

To take this further, many inexperienced fighters will not only telegraph their attack with a step, but will also at the same time start setting up their body position for the *type* of kick they are about to deliver. This is as good as verbally telling your opponent what you are about to do, and helps him not only to defend against it but also to plan his counter-attack.

Most of the time when you punch you will push off using the back leg at the same time, to cover distance and add power to the attack. A step here works because the lead leg is in such a position that it can support the body properly as you land. Also, you do not need to change your centre of balance as you are not lifting your lead leg off the floor. When you kick, however, you are lifting a leg off the floor and, if your stance is too wide, this becomes near impossible – just try it.

In learning to perform a hop step, first make sure that your stance is not too long. Start with your rear leg positioned directly underneath your rear shoulder (Fig 507). You can set this up simply enough and without your opponent noticing by

Fig 507 Face your opponent.

Fig 508 Bring the lead leg off the floor.

Fig 509 Hop forwards off the back leg.

Fig 510 Land the hop front kick.

using your footwork as you are moving around in your fighting stance. From here, bring the kicking leg off the floor (Fig 508). This movement is exaggerated in Fig 508 for the purposes of clarity, but

Fig 511 Bring your lead leg off the floor.

you actually need to bring your foot off the floor by only a few millimetres. If you fail to bring your foot off the floor initially as you learn this move, you will be tempted to step up with your rear leg.

As you bring your lead foot off the floor, hop forwards, springing off your rear leg (Fig 509), and land the kick at the same time as your rear leg lands (Fig 510). This simple movement will enable you to cover distance (the greater the hop, the more distance covered) and add power to your attack in exactly the same way as would a step off your rear leg. The beauty of the hop step, however, is that your opponent will not know what is coming as you are not telegraphing the kick.

To start with, the hop-step technique will feel very unnatural and you probably will not be able to cover much distance or deliver any power at all. Do persist with it, practising initially on a heavy bag or kick shield before attempting it for real. Once you can competently pull this simple movement off, it is guaranteed to change the way you kick for ever.

The hop step can be adapted to work with any of the static kicks, the most common ones being the front, round, side and axe kicks. The technique will not work, however, with any of the spinning

Fig 512 Hop forwards.

Fig 513 Side kick to the exposed area.

kicks, so do not waste your time trying. Instead, focus your energies on learning how to use this step with the basic kicks, and on the stages you have to go through to change the core body of the kick for all the different kicks, from a front kick through to an axe kick, for example.

Using the hop step with a side kick will help you to understand better the rising side kick drill (*see* pages 178–9), and also the way in which you need to adjust the body to ensure it is in the correct position for the successful delivery of the kick you are planning to use.

In your fighting stance, lift your lead foot off the floor in preparation for the attack (Fig 511). Hop forwards using the rear leg and, as you do so, chamber the kick (Fig 512), then land the kick and the hop at the same time (Fig 513).

Advanced Level Training Drills

This stage will give the big kickers out there some high-level kicking drills to take away and play with. For beginner and intermediate level students, this is the level to which you should ultimately aspire if you want to say that you truly understand your kicks. Be aware though that you will get out of this what you put into it. If high-level kicking is something you would like to be able to do (and it will give you a great advantage over the fighter who does not fully understand the kick), you must be prepared to spend many hours on this section.

The Round Kick–Hook Kick Combo

From your fighting stance, send out a lead-leg round kick to the head (Fig 514). As your opponent blocks the kick, re-chamber the leg (Fig 515), adjust your hip position (Fig 516), and hook kick to the opposite side of the head (Fig 517).

Although this combo may appear slow in the figures, in reality, with a little practice, it can be very fast. The trick with it is to send out the round kick with some power. This will ensure that your opponent puts more emphasis on his defence, which will buy you an extra millisecond (a serious amount of time in a fight) in which to change your attack. It might even be worth sending out a single power round kick first as your opponent will

Fig 514 Round kick to the head to distract from the second kick.

Fig 515 Re-chamber the leg.

Fig 516 Extend the kicking leg out.

then ensure he blocks your second one, allowing himself to be set up in this way.

If he happens to cover both sides of his head, you simply switch your second attack to a side kick (*see* page 182, 'The Round Kick Side Kick Combo'). If he keeps his elbows tight together so that a side kick would not land, then send out a front kick to drive his defence apart. Again, the skill here is being able to switch your strategy in an instant and without missing a beat, taking into account how your opponent has now reacted to your initial attack.

The Axe Kick–Side Kick Combo

Send out a lead-leg axe kick to the head of your opponent. Your intention here is to bait your partner into blocking the attack and exposing his body (Fig 518). As soon as the kick is blocked, pull the leg back and chamber it for a side kick (Fig 519) striking to the body as it remains unguarded (Fig 520).

The Side Kick–Axe Kick Combo

Send out a side kick to the body of your opponent. This should result in him covering up to prevent the

Fig 517 Hook kick to the exposed area.

Fig 518 Lead axe kick to the head to open up the opponent's body.

Fig 519 Chamber the leg for a side kick.

Fig 520 Side kick to the exposed area.

kick from landing (Fig 521). Bounce the side kick off his guard (Fig 522) and, from here, straighten the leg so it extends over your opponent's blind shoulder, and drive it back down, targeting the head if it is still exposed (Fig 523).

Fig 521 Side kick to the body to bring the guard down.

Fig 522 Re-chamber the leg for an axe kick.

The Spinning Hook–Kick Round Kick Combo

From your fighting stance (Fig 524), twist your body backwards (Fig 525) and send out a spinning hook kick to your opponent's head (Fig 526). As spinning kicks on their own are relatively easy to see coming, this should result in your opponent leaning out of the way of the kick, if he does not attempt to block it. As the kick passes in front of him, stop it at this point (Fig 527) and fire out a round kick to the opposite side of his head (Fig 528).

The bonus here is that your opponent will probably expect you to land your leg once your spinning kicks misses and he may well try to take advantage of this by attempting to rush in for a counter-punch. If he does, it is highly likely that, if you time it right, your round kick will find its mark.

Triple Kick Combo

Of course, you can group together as many kicks as you want before landing your leg, but any more

Fig 523 Axe kick to the exposed area.

Fig 524 Face your opponent.

Fig 525 Start the spinning hook kick.

Fig 526 Stop the kick as it passes the centre line.

Fig 527 Chamber the leg.

Fig 528 Round kick to the head.

than three (though you might just get away with four) will probably result in you over-committing to your attack. Fighters will often panic when a kicking combo does not work and then try to over-compensate by continuing the attack, for fear that, if they land their leg, their opponent will find his mark. The opponent usually regains his composure after the first two kicks fail to land, side-steps and lands a successful counter to the blind side, as the kicker desperately tries to make good his hashed attempt at a multiple-kick attack.

If you are going to experiment with multiple kicking combos, choose your kicks wisely. Some flow more naturally together than others so you need to ensure that, whichever attacks you use, the energy of one seamlessly carries you on to the next one.

From your fighting stance (Fig 529), hook kick to the head of your opponent (Fig 530). As he evades the kick, re-chamber it (Fig 531) and send out a round kick to the body (Fig 532), then re-chamber it (Fig 533) and send out a round kick to the head (Fig 534).

191

Fig 529 Face your opponent.

Fig 530 Hook kick to the head.

Fig 531 Chamber the leg.

Fig 532 Round kick to the body.

Fig 533 Re-chamber the leg.

Fig 534 Strike to the head.

Spinning Hook Kick Set-Up

This final combination will help you to understand how to set up a spinning kick successfully. Spinning kicks can bring great results, but most people do not really know how to use them. Inexperienced fighters often attempt to perform random spinning kicks, either for effect or because they genuinely believe they can land them. This can be dangerous and, if they happen to be facing a more experienced fighter at the time, can certainly cost them the fight (if not more).

The spinning kick needs to be set up correctly and there are two general rules:

1 Time an attack from your opponent and send out the most appropriate spinning kick based on the attack that you receive (*see* page 141, 'Counters Against Punches Using Kicks'). Your timing can either be used to beat him to the attack as he telegraphs his intentions, or to counter his attack once you have evaded or blocked it and he is attempting to recover.
2 Using a combination of techniques, set up a

spinning-kick attack to affect your opponent's defence and body position, and to disguise the fact that you are about to spin. The problems of telegraphing a technique (*see* page 73) are easily appreciated when you witness a less experienced fighter attempting to perform a circular spinning kick.

From your fighting stance, send out a fast jab to the head to bring the guard up (Fig 535). Straight away, send a cross punch down to the mid line, twisting your body as you do to set up the next attack (Fig 536). Drive back up and lead hook to the head, starting the twisting motion for the spinning kick (Fig 537). From here, continue through with the spin, keeping your foot on the floor until the very last minute (Fig 538), and drive the kick round to the head of your opponent (Fig 539).

There are of course many combinations that you could use to set up a spinning kick, which will depend on whether the kick is a straight-through spinning kick (as in the case of a spinning back kick, for example) or a circular spinning kick (as with this

193

Fig 535 Send out a jab to bring the guard up ...

one). Practise this one for now and when you become comfortable with the transition from hooking punch to spinning kick, and you are able to do it without giving away what you are building up to, you can then start adding in your own combos.

How to Train these Drills

Strict training drills, coupled with timings and rest periods, are not given here because, if you are ready to start sparring, you should already have a good enough understanding of how to work a drill, based on your normal training sessions. If you do not completely understand how to train a specific drill, there is also a chance that you are not yet proficient enough with your basic technical ability. Your foundations really need to be up to a high enough standard to get you through a sparring bout before you venture into this uncharted territory.

Fig 536 ... cross to the exposed area ...

Fig 537 ... and hook to set up the spinning kick ...

Fig 538 ... Start the spin ...

Fig 539 ... and kick to the exposed area.

If you are capable of putting together your own set of timings and drills, do not forget the following rules:

- The length of time you set for a drill needs to be directly proportionate to your fitness level, allowing for enough overlap to push you. It is no good doing a drill for just 30 seconds if you are a black belt student.
- Try varying your drills by setting both a time duration and a number duration – in other words, perform twenty drills on one side, instead of 2 minutes on the timer, for example. It is very easy to end up performing only five drills in 2 minutes if you take your time.
- Vary your training session so that you can work on your own using the appropriate apparatus (shadowing, mirror work, punchbag, speed

ball, maize ball, ping pong ball and so on), and with a training partner (holding kick shields, focus pads, time-allocated sessions, one-for-one training drills, technical sparring, for example).
- Vary your training partners so you do not become accustomed to fighting only a certain size, height and body type. Ensure you train with taller training partners, smaller training partners, heavier and lighter ones, male and female ones, faster and slower, less experienced and more experienced.
- Ensure that any rest period is directly proportionate to your ability; if you rest for too long, you will start to cool down. Ideally, the shorter the rest period the better, as this will get you used to recovering more quickly, which in turn will help you to develop more rapidly.

- Train with a heart monitor and record your progress over a period of time. This will help you to see how quickly you are progressing. Try removing the stopwatch and replacing it with the heart monitor, finishing and restarting the drill when your heartbeat reaches a certain level; for example, when it reaches 160bpm you stop, and when it reaches 120bpm you restart.

Have fun with these drills and be sure to work to your pace when setting your training times and routines. Remember that the more successful method of training is to do it little and often, as opposed to one big session every now and again.

14 Point Sparring

Point sparring is a popular style of fighting associated with many of the sport-related martial arts such as free-style kickboxing, sport karate and certain styles of taekwon-do and kung fu. It differs from continuous sparring in that the fighters do not fight continuously, scoring points for successful attacks as they go. Instead, they look to score isolated points throughout the fight, with the winner accumulating the most individual points at the end of the bout.

This time the referees' job is slightly different, with the main referee relying on the eyes of at least one other shadow referee standing opposite to confirm that the attacks have landed on the scoring zones. In the bigger tournaments there will normally be three referees in total – one main ref and two shadow refs. When a clean attack is witnessed by at least two referees, the main ref will stop the fight, instruct the fighters to return to their marks (starting positions), and award the points accordingly. The score-keeper will then add the points to a visual display, either electronic or flip card, and the referee will start the fight again.

Despite the apparent rest period, point fighting, when done competitively, is an incredibly demanding discipline, requiring good stamina and cardio-vascular fitness. The key to a successful point fighter is a good understanding of speed and timing. Speed, and in particular explosive speed, is key, as the faster the fighter can move from his starting position to the attack the greater the chance of the technique landing. For that reason, unlike the continuous bouts, in which each opponent may throw many techniques in any one attack, a point fighter will rarely throw more than two or three techniques at any one time, but each attack will be explosive and lightning fast.

The other difference between the point fighter and the continuous fighter is that the point fighter may take bigger risks when committing to an attack. Providing your attack lands first, and the referee sees it of course, it does not really matter if your opponent catches you afterwards; it is your initial attack that, if successful, will score. Therefore, a point fighter can sometimes risk getting hit on the exchange providing his attack is seen to land first. In the continuous game, however, this approach could cost you the fight, particularly in full-contact bouts. As a result, the continuous fighter is likely to be a little more reserved about simply rushing in to attack, whereas the point fighter can afford to take that calculated gamble.

Anyone who has ever witnessed a top-level point fighter in action cannot fail to be blown away by the speed and energy of these incredible athletes. And anyone who thinks it is the easier of the two fighting styles need only try it for themselves to understand that it can be as physically demanding as any continuous bout, particularly as full-contact point competitions are now slowly making their way on to the tournament scene.

The following simple drills for the point fighter, divided into beginner, intermediate and advanced levels, can be used for either semi-contact or even full-contact point fighting. The key when training for point fighting is to focus on explosive techniques that can work well either on their own due to their nature, or in combination with one or two other techniques that can be used to set up a blitz-style attack.

Beginner Level Drills

There are a number of simple explosive techniques that can be used on their own to perform lightning-fast attacks. These drills do require a good understanding of projectile movement and, when combined with speed and timing, the isolated techniques can be so fast that the opponent may not even see them coming.

Gloves

The gloves worn for point fighting differ from the gloves worn for continuous fighting. Continuous fighters generally wear more of a boxing-style glove, resulting in a greater level of protection to both the puncher and the opponent. The point fighter tends to wear more of a lighter-weight glove, which also aids his speed of movement. Currently the vast majority of point competitions are light- or semi-contact, so the point fighter does not necessarily need to afford the same level of protection to his opponent as those participating in a full-contact continuous bout, for example.

Fig 540 shows an example of the type of glove worn by a point fighter.

Fig 540 Point sparring gloves.

The Explosive Backfist Strike

The backfist strike is possibly the fastest technique in the kickboxer's repertoire and, if done properly, can be used to strike an opponent before he has time to react. The key with the backfist strike is to set up the technique correctly and fully commit to the attack, otherwise you run the risk of your attack being countered by your opponent.

In your fighting stance, bring your lead hand slightly forward of your guard so that it is unnoticeably nearer to your opponent. The aim of this set-up is to remove the gap between your fist and your opponent, thereby reducing the overall time it takes for the technique to land, as it has less distance to travel – but without your opponent seeing what you are doing. Try practising this sleight of hand as you shadow or perform your mirror work to see how, with a bit of training, it can be almost unnoticeable to your opponent. Fig 541 shows how the lead hand has now moved away from the traditional guard position into the ready position for the attack.

From here, push off with your rear foot, transferring all your body weight on to your lead foot as you project yourself forwards towards your opponent (Fig 542). The best way to describe the energy required for this part of the attack is to think of yourself as a sprinter exploding off the blocks. Imagine yourself sprinting forwards with the intention of running through your opponent. At the same time, whip your backfist out, aiming to hit the side of your opponent's head and, at the last minute, step through with your rear leg to stop yourself from falling face first on to the floor (Fig 543).

It will take a little practice to get used to this way of performing a backfist strike, however, once you can explode like this, the chances of it landing are greatly increased. Combine this with 100 per cent commitment as well as great timing and you suddenly have a weapon that you can add to your arsenal that will be effective most of the time.

To help you develop this technique, try practising it on a punch bag, a partner while sparring and also while holding focus pads and a smaller target such as a speed ball, or similar striking target. The key to developing the explosive speed you need for this and most of the techniques involved in point sparring is of course practice, practice, practice.

Fig 541 Face your opponent.

Fig 542 Push off your rear foot.

Fig 543 Hit with the backfist strike.

The Explosive Jab

This is another incredibly fast technique that employs the same principles as the explosive backfist. From your fighting stance (Fig 544), push off with your rear foot as you project yourself forward towards your opponent. At the same time, snap the jab out, aiming at the mid line (Fig 545).

This attack can also be used to target the head, but with a word of warning: straight punches of this nature, when used to attack the face, are generally frowned upon (if not illegal in some tournaments). With so much force behind it (your whole body is now behind the punch), there is an inherent chance that the strike will border more on the full-contact side, which, given the style of the gloves you are wearing, will result not only in a warning for excessive contact (which could result in a disqualification) but also in the risk of you seriously injuring your opponent.

When employing these types of attack in a sport environment, it is advisable to respect your opponent and target more of the body (chest and stomach), as he is likely to be better able to absorb an attack of this nature than a hit full on in the face.

Fig 544 Face your opponent.

Fig 545 Push off your rear foot.

Fig 546 Jab to the body.

Fig 547 Alternative view showing the guard.

You are still likely to get the point, you stand less chance of being jeered by the crowd, and the law of karma remains equally balanced and ready for the next round.

As the punch lands, step through with your rear leg to assist with your balance, and be sure to cover your head as your opponent will now attempt to counter your punch with one of his own, regardless of whether your punch landed first or not (Fig 546). Fig 547 shows the guard slightly better when viewed on the opposite side.

The Explosive Cross

The same principles apply to the explosive cross as they do for the explosive jab. The only real difference here is that you are just twisting the body more in the opposite direction to allow for the extra reach required to land that cross punch. As before, it is recommended that you attack the body more with this attack; if the body is not available, you need to know how to make it available (*see* the next drill). Figs 548 and 549 show this attack in motion.

The Backfist–Cross Punch Combo

This is a two-fold drill – you can either use the initial attack to bait the opponent into opening up his mid line (in this case, it is the second attack that you actually want to land), or you attempt to attack with the first technique, but, when your opponent manages to block, you quickly switch your intentions and send out a second attack while they are on the back foot.

It is often said that, if you want to hit someone in the head, first set out to hit them in the body. This refers to the fact that, if you attack the body the opponent will, in most cases, naturally bring his guard down to defend his body against this attack. As this happens, there is a slight chance that he will leave the head unguarded, which could buy enough time for you to send a second attack up to this area.

The same principle works the other way round. As you attack the head, your opponent may bring his guard up to defend against your attack, thereby exposing the mid line for a brief second. This exposure could be enough for you to land a successful second attack to the body. From your

Fig 548 Face your opponent.

Fig 549 Explode in with a cross to the body.

fighting stance (Fig 550), send out a backfist strike to the head (Fig 551). The second your opponent blocks the attack, send out a cross punch to the body (Fig 552).

Your opponent will have a number of possible options in response to this combination:

- He may attempt to move back instead of block-ing your attack. A fully committed backfist, cross-punch attack with forward movement should still find its mark if done with 100 per cent commitment.
- Instead of using a lead rising block to defend the backfist strike, he may try to parry it. If so, your second attack should still land as the parry will focus on the first attack, exposing an area of the body for the second attack to target.
- He may bring his arms up and use a forearm-style block to defend the backfist. This should still result in an exposure of the mid line, allow-ing the cross punch to sneak in.

The key to understanding this type of attack is to think of the whole attack as an explosion. If you aim to send out a backfist and cross punch togeth-er, then there is a greater chance of your attack landing. Where you will fall down with this attack is when you pause between the backfist strike and the cross punch. That pause, against a skilled opponent, provides enough of a gap for him to counter your attack.

Think of your attacks now as a series of beats. The first beat is the backfist and the second beat is the cross punch. If you add in a third beat, it becomes backfist, pause, cross punch, and it is this additional beat that will cost you the point. Study the sequence again (Figs 550–552). The cross punch has landed while the backfist is still in play. The backfist has not been retracted to create a clearer path for the cross punch to travel down, or to create a guard again for you to cover your-self with. In the game of point fighting there is not enough time for this.

Keeping the backfist in play will do two things:

1 It will speed up the overall attack
2 It will prevent the opponent from using this arm to counter with.

Fig 550 Face your opponent.

Fig 551 Backfist to the head to draw the guard up.

Fig 552 Cross to the open area.

Note how the backfist strike now obstructs your opponent's lead arm, preventing him from using it, and how the forearm of the same arm also doubles as a defence giving cover to your head. This is why you need to believe fully in your attack and commit to it 100 per cent. Any hesitation or doubt will result in a half-hearted, slow attack, which will naturally be defended and countered by a more confident opponent, ultimately costing you the fight.

The Cross Punch–Backfist Combo

This combination is simply the reverse of the previous one, only this time you want to attack the head, so you first set off to attack the body. It is always worthwhile having several good combinations to hand that work well for you as it is highly likely that your opponent will get wise to your attacks if you use the same one throughout the fight. This way, you can alternate between several totally different attacks and in that way your opponent has a harder time of trying to work you out.

In your fighting stance (Fig 553), send out a cross punch to the body (Fig 554). If the punch

Fig 553 Face your opponent.

Fig 554 The cross is blocked.

203

Fig 555 Backfist to the head.

lands (and the ref sees it), you get the bonus of the point for that attack. However, if your opponent blocks the attack, or if you bait him with it (intending for him to block it), then from here you can send a backfist strike up to the head (Fig 555).

The same rule applies: throw this combination using just two beats by keeping the cross punch where it is as you send out the backfist strike. Retracting the punch will cost you a beat and could result in a successful counter-strike from your opponent.

It is probably worth spending some quality time training these drills, before moving on to the next section, even if you do consider yourself to be at a higher level. This is because the way you explode into the simple attacks will help you understand exactly how every attack, when competing as a point fighter, needs to be executed. Follow the example of the full-contact kickboxing world champion, whose training regime as he prepares for a title fight involves hours of point-fighting training, just to help him maintain his ability to explode into every kick and punch. He puts a lot

of his success down to the fact that he can instantly attack, regardless of his position, with incredible speed and timing.

Anyone thinking that point fighting is a simple game of 'flick and tag' is in for a big surprise. Regardless of the style of fighting you choose to study – based on standing, ground, weapons, sport or reality, if you can deliver your attacks faster than your opponent can, you stand a very good chance of walking away victorious.

Intermediate Level Drills

These drills introduce you to the ridge-hand strike, as well as incorporating a few kicks into the attacks. It is important for a good point fighter to be able to switch between kicks and punches, and not get caught in that trap of relying solely on hand speed to win the fight. The ability to kick well is of equal importance, as the kick should be the weapon of choice when you are out of the punching range. They are also incredibly effective when it comes to closing the gap and bringing you into the punching range. Many fighters neglect their kicking as it takes a considerable amount of conscious effort to develop in this area. It is much easier to throw out a punch and although there is an significant amount of skill involved when it comes to using the hands, why would you not want to have the choice to kick if that was the better technique at a particular moment?

The Jab–Lead Ridge Hand Combo
This blitz-style attack works by utilizing a double attack with the same hand. This combo is very effective, but you will have to be able to explode with both shots as you will need to retract the hand once the first attack is blocked.

In your fighting stance (Fig 556), explode in with a jab to the body. Do not be tempted to jab to the head with this attack, even if you are planning on controlling the power, as this will just set your opponent up to cover the target area of our second attack. Once the jab is blocked (Fig 557), retract the arm slightly (Fig 558) and instantly send out a ridge-hand strike to the side of the head (Fig 559).

The key thing to understand with this attack is that the retraction is only a half retraction – you are

Fig 556 Face your opponent.

Fig 557 The jab is blocked.

not pulling the jab back to the guard. If you were to do this you would increase the gap between the attack and the target, which of course would buy your opponent some time. Instead, pull the arm back only enough to clear it away from the opponent's block (in this case the rear-hand parry) and, as his blocking arm continues to move, immediately send the second attack on its way.

Fig 558 Chamber the arm for a ridge-hand strike.

Fig 559 Ridge hand to the head.

The Ridge-Hand Strike

The ridge-hand strike is not always featured in every kickboxing syllabus; Fig 560 shows it in action. The hand is positioned flat instead of clenched in a fist. The thumb is tucked tightly into the palm, to avoid damaging it, and the elbow of the striking arm remains slightly bent to prevent over-extension of the joint as the ridge hand hits.

The technique travels in a circular motion from the outside in, similar to that of a hooking punch and although the whole of the hand will make the connection with the target, the actual striking part is the side knuckle of the index finger.

Fig 560 The hand position for a ridge-hand strike.

The Cross Punch–Lead Ridge-Hand Combo

This combination is quite effective as it uses body mechanics to set up the second attack. In your fighting stance (Fig 561), send out a cross punch

Fig 561 Face your opponent.

Fig 562 The cross punch is blocked.

to the body (Fig 562). As you cross punch, fully commit to the attack and, without over-extending your punch, ensure that you project through with your striking arm, turning the body slightly to help bridge the gap between you and your opponent. As soon as the punch is blocked, immediately send out a ridge-hand strike to the side of the head while you bring your opposite hand up to form a guard – just in case (Fig 563).

The Backfist–Axe Kick Combo

This combination is a great one to use when you have the opponent on the back foot, so to speak. If used correctly, the opponent actually steps or leans back into the kick so its success rate, with good training, is very high.

In a fighting stance (Fig 564), explode with a backfist strike towards your opponent (Fig 565). An experienced fighter may lean or step back to avoid getting caught, while, against a less experienced fighter, the backfist may land. As your opponent leans back, step through with your rear leg to set up the kick (Fig 566), use the momentum of

Fig 563 Lead ridge hand to the head.

Fig 564 Face your opponent.

Fig 565 The backfist is evaded.

Fig 566 Step through with your rear leg.

Fig 567 Chamber the leg for an axe kick.

Fig 568 Execute the axe kick.

the step to swing the kicking leg up (Fig 567), and drive the axe kick down on to the target (Fig 568).

The Cross Punch–Rear Ridge-Hand Strike Combo

This combo works along the same lines as the jab–lead ridge-hand combo, except that you are now working the combo off the rear side. There are many reasons why you might use this combo off the rear hand but it could mainly be because of your body position just before you attack. Understanding where your centre of balance is, how you are positioned and where your energy is coming from all go towards deciding how to attack your opponent. The skill of course is removing the conscious thought process from the equation and, instead of thinking about it, simply reacting.

Square up to your opponent (Fig 569). Cross punch to the body in order to bring the guard down (Fig 570). As your opponent blocks the attack, retract the hand (Fig 571) and strike to the head (Fig 572).

Fig 569 Face your opponent.

Fig 570 The cross is blocked.

Fig 571 Chamber the hand for the ridge hand.

Fig 572 Rear ridge-hand strike to the head.

Fig 573 Face your opponent.

Fig 574 The backfist is blocked.

Fig 575 Chamber the leg for a side kick.

Fig 576 The side kick lands.

The Backfist–Side Kick Combo

This combination involves setting up a kick from the punching range. In order for this combination to work you will need to adjust your body position by leaning away from the opponent, to ensure you can fit the kick in. It is a slight movement (see Figs 573–576), but it needs to be quick and this is assisted by not moving the supporting leg in between the attacks.

Face your opponent in a fighting stance (Fig 573). Send out the backfist strike to the head, which your opponent blocks (Fig 574). As your opponent exposes his mid line, bring your kicking leg straight up by pushing off the front foot and chambering the leg for the side kick (Fig 575). From here it is a simple case of snapping out the kick to find its target (Fig 576).

In the sequence, it may look as though there is a time delay between chambering the kick and striking, but the actual movement from bringing the leg off the floor and striking needs to take just milliseconds. Again, this is where your ability to explode into a technique comes in.

Fig 577 Face your opponent.

Advanced Level Drills

The following drills practise advanced-level techniques that can be used when point sparring. They are aimed at students with a good understanding of the higher-level techniques and of body mechanics, energy and timing. You also need to be able to put it all together so you can actually perform the technique – understanding is one thing but ability to perform is another.

If you are already at this level, off you go. However, if you are not yet there, it is advisable to wait until you are before trying these techniques for real. It is better to spend the next twelve months practising them so that you can pull them off without effort than to make the common rookie mistake of trying them too soon, because they look 'cool', and then to fall flat on your face (metaphorically speaking) in the heat of the fight. Practice makes permanent, so they say.

Backfist–Jumping Back Kick Combo

The various kicks (spinning back kick, jumping spinning back kick, and so on) are well worth

Fig 578 The backfist is blocked.

Fig 579 Twist the body for back kick.

Fig 580 The jumping back kick lands.

getting to know. Not only are they incredibly powerful and work well but also, if they land, they can literally stop the fight. Even if this sort of kick is blocked, it will still buy you a second to recover from the jump and/or send out another attack as your opponent will also need to recover from the impact. The other reason why these kicks are so useful is because, even if they are blocked, your leg acts as a natural barrier between you and your opponent, so he has a limited possibility of rushing in to attack you immediately – providing, of course, that the kick is performed properly.

From your fighting stance (Fig 577), send out a backfist strike to engage your opponent and to lure him into bringing his guard up and exposing his mid line (Fig 578). Almost as soon as you have attacked with the backfist, twist round (Fig 579) and send out the jumping back kick to the exposed area (Fig 580). The jumping version of this kick tends to be a little faster than the spinning version and the energy of the jump helps to add that little extra 'kick' to the technique. As you start learning this combo, it might be that you

need to begin with the spinning kick before progressing on to the jumping version.

The Spinning Hook Kick–Jab Combo

You see many inexperienced (and some experienced) fighters attempting to throw circular spinning kicks straight off the mark, without attempting to use a combination or even just good timing to set them up. If you are up against an experienced fighter, rarely will you see one of these kicks land; for that reason, you really need to set up this type of kick, or at least use it with good timing to counter a sloppy attack from your opponent.

On that note, however, it is possible to use a spinning hook kick to set up a second attack or even recover from a mistimed spinning attack with this type of combination. If you think about it, it is easier to see a kick coming than it is to see a punch as the hand is already much closer to your opponent than the foot is (particularly if you are aiming for the head). Similarly, it is easier to see a spinning kick coming than a lead-leg kick, as the rear foot is even further away. Therefore, as you attempt to

Fig 581 Face your opponent.

Fig 582 Twist the body for a spinning hook kick.

Fig 583 The kick is evaded.

Fig 584 Bring the lead hand into position.

Fig 585 The jab lands.

attack with your spinning-kick combo, your opponent has much more time to react to it, and where circular spinning kicks are concerned, this is what generally happens. The difference is that, this time, you are going to use it to your advantage.

In your fighting stance (Fig 581), twist your body round to start the kick (Fig 582). As you hook your leg towards your opponent's head, there's a very good chance your opponent will simply lean back out of the way of your attack (Fig 583). As he sees you starting to land the leg back down again, he may try to rush in with a counter-strike to catch you off balance. Ensure that at this point you are leaning slightly into the attack and your body mechanics are correct, otherwise your punch may fall short (Fig 584). As your lead hand comes back round to the front, drive a jab out to either the body or head of your opponent depending on what is available at the time (Fig 585).

As you should know, normally when performing a spinning kick of this nature, you ideally want to keep your head back and out of the way of a possible counter-strike from your opponent.

However, as you intend to strike immediately after this initial attack, on this occasion you need to change the body position slightly to ensure the jab reaches.

The Double Spinning Kick Combo

It is always a good idea to follow up after performing a spinning attack as the experienced fighter will wait for you to slip up with one of these and counter your attack as you are attempting to recover. If you do not have a second attack ready there is a good chance that your opponent will use it to his advantage. This next technique takes the follow-up attack a stage further.

In your fighting stance (Fig 586), start the twisting motion for the kick (Fig 587) and perform the spinning hook kick as before (Fig 588). Now, instead of landing the leg back round to where it started from, as you would normally, stop the leg dead and drop it straight down so it lands in front (Fig 589). Then readjust your body position and start a reverse spin (you may find this easier with a little step across using your front

Fig 586 Face your opponent.

Fig 587 Twist the body for a spinning hook kick.

Fig 588 The kick is evaded.

Fig 589 Land the leg in front.

Fig 590 Spin back round the opposite way.

Fig 591 The other leg lands.

Fig 592 Face your opponent.

leg). Fig 590 shows this move quite clearly. From here, simply spin back the other way, striking with a spinning hook kick off your other leg this time (Fig 591).

Fake Axe Kick–Round Kick Combo

This combination uses a fake (or feint) to lead your opponent into opening up his guard, by making him believe that your intentions are different from what they actually are. As simple as this combination may appear, there is actually a considerable level of skill involved in setting up the initial attack and seamlessly switching it mid-flow before your opponent has time to react.

In your fighting stance (Fig 592), start bringing your lead leg up as if you were about to perform an axe kick. Ideally, when performing an axe kick in this way, you keep the leg slightly bent but still go through the full range of motion to let your opponent think you are about to execute a full-blown kick (Fig 593). As you see your opponent preparing to block the kick, switch your hip position, changing the kick mid-flow, and chambering

Fig 593 Chamber the leg for an axe kick.

Fig 594 Switch the leg for a round kick.

Fig 595 Round kick to the body ...

the leg for a round kick (Fig 594). From here it is a simple case of snapping the kick out to either the body (Fig 595) or the head (Fig 596), based on what is open at the time.

Fig 596 ... or to the head if open.

15 Final Words

I have been teaching and writing about kickboxing and martial arts now for many years and the one question I get asked all the time is, 'How do I develop the box splits?' I'm the first to admit that the best way of showing off your flexibility is a full box-split stretch and most practitioners of flexibility-based pastimes do strive to achieve this coveted goal. However, my answer is always the same. In our game (fighting), you do not actually need to be able to perform the box splits in order to reach the head of most fighters.

If your chosen area in the martial arts is creative forms (or 'musical forms', 'free forms', 'extreme forms', or whatever it is they are calling them now), then an impressive 180-degree split kick is certainly going to turn heads, but, as a fighter, do you really need to kick that high? If you do ever come across an opponent that tall, the last thing you would be advised to do is try and kick them in the head anyway.

If you look again at the head-height kicks described here (for example, Fig 596), you will clearly see that none actually involves a full splits position and yet they still manage to reach the head of the opponent with relative ease. Certainly, do not stop developing your flexibility and if, in time, you achieve a box-split stretch, then you can go ahead and tick that box. However, it is not worth putting your training on hold and missing out on many years of self-development, character-building and of course enjoyment (which is ultimately what it is about) by focusing on something only a few feet ahead of you. That would be like waiting until you are fit enough to start training before you start training.

Kickboxing, martial arts, reality training and self-defence are all rewarding hobbies for some, but they represent a lifetime's study for others. Whether you are in it for the long term or just stopping off for a quick look as you continue on your journey to find whatever it is you are looking for, I wish you luck with your quest. I started my journey at the tender age of fourteen and it is a journey that is still ongoing. The martial arts have given me an incredible life, kept me on the right path and are now able to give me back a little of

Fig 597 Andrew and Colin fight it out in a Blaze club tournament.

Fig 598 The side kick finds its mark.

the investment that I have put in. I can confidently say that it has been life-changing.

When I started training, the martial arts were just starting to become commercialized. Judo and karate had dominated the scene for quite some time and taekwon-do was just becoming a household name. Mixed Martial Arts (MMA) was totally unheard of and, although a few of the most hardened martial artists might have trained in a couple of different arts, to fight competitively using more than one style was something that no one would have even considered. The nearest we ever got to it was entering an open competition where you might get freestyle fighters from karate, taekwon-do, kickboxing and kung fu under the same roof.

Similarly, the thought of being paid to fight never even entered our heads and was often only talked about by dreamers during conversations that started with, 'Wouldn't it be great if...'. I do remember my karate instructor many years ago telling me that he believed that one day we would have millionaires born through their ability to fight. Back then it was only really top-level boxing that created such wealth and if you liked to kick (and I enjoyed a good kick as much as the next person), you were pretty much stuck with what you had.

Two decades later, there are hundreds of schools all over the country teaching mixed martial arts, packed full of students of every calibre (not all of them studying for the right reasons). There are tournaments of every style, shape and size every weekend and, if that is not enough for you, you can always take on the world. With cash prizes to be won at most events, if you enter a tournament now and the top prize is a tiny plastic trophy then it can be a little disappointing.

With world-class instructors on your doorstep and thanks to events such as the UFC (Ultimate Fighting Championships), Pride and the many hundreds of others too numerous to mention, we are today seeing fighters become millionaires through martial arts. And with sponsorship deals bigger than ever, training easier to come by, and technology as it is now, it is a great time to be getting into the hobby. I wish I could have my time over again!

But it is a dog-eat-dog world and you only get out of it what you put in. Is success guaranteed for everyone? Surely not, otherwise we would all be world champions or millionaires. Is it guaranteed for you? Possibly, if you really understand and appreciate what it takes. If you want the wealth, the fame, the recognition and everything that comes with it, you have to be prepared to give before you get. Alternatively, if the highest level is not for you, there is no reason why you cannot still enjoy your training, achieve a good standard, and still experience all the life-changing benefits that a martial art can give you. Then again, one day you might receive your first punch in the face, call time, take your gloves off and never venture into a kickboxing school again.

Regardless of what you do decide to do, I hope you understand my message and find it inspiring. Let me leave you with one more thought. There is much debate in the martial-art world over which is the best style, the best technique, the best punch, kick, and so on. Yet in almost every sport-based fight I have seen over the years, there is normally one winner and one loser. If they both study the same fighting style and both hold the same rank, does this mean it is the individual or the style that is the ultimate deciding factor? You could argue that there were factors on the day that contributed to the outcome but, if they fight more than once and the same fighter wins every time, then what is the answer?

Fig 599 Four of our junior members bringing home the trophies.